MW01089533

All About Money

A compilation of financial columns by Steve Nicklas published from 1994-2011.

Library of Congress Cataloging-in-Publication Data

Nicklas, Steve
       All About Money: A Compilation of Financial Columns/ Steve
Nicklas
       p. cm.
       Does not include index.
       1.   Financial columns published between 1994-2011. I. Title

Copyright © 2011 by Steve Nicklas

All rights reserved.

No part of this book may be reproduced in any form or by any
electronic or mechanical means including information storage and
retrieval systems, without permission in writing from the author. The
only exception is by a reviewer, who may quote short excerpts in a
review.

This publication is designed to provide accurate and authoritative
information in regard to the subject matter covered. It is sold with the
understanding that the author and publisher are not engaged in
rendering legal, accounting or other professional service. If legal
advice or other expert assistance is required, the services of a
competent professional person should be sought. The author and
publisher specifically disclaim any liability that is incurred from the
use or application of the contents of this book.

-       *From a declaration of principles jointly adopted by a
        committee of the American Bar Association and a committee
        of publishers*

ISBN-13: **978-1482561654** (CreateSpace-Assigned)

I hope you enjoy this eclectic compilation of financial columns I've written over the last 17 years. Each column is prefaced by the date of publication in the Fernandina Beach News-Leader – and in other newspapers of the New York Times Regional Newspaper Group and of Community Newspapers, Inc.

These columns are built on foundations of facts, which are then intertwined with my interpretations and opinions. Some columns are more factual; others are more opinion. Still others are controversial, or sentimental, or uplifting. But most have a message, a statement, reverting back to something about money. After all, when our lives – here and around the world – are distilled into a basic element, a necessity, it becomes *all about money*.

Table of Contents

5

Part One: Politics

Hoping for Better Government /March 2007

If there is an informal movement to clean house within the Nassau County government, the cleaning may nearly be complete -- with spic-and-span quality and speed.

In the latest cleansing, Mike Mahaney has been removed from the vital county administrator position after several years in office. Mahaney apparently lost the confidence of his bosses, who are the county commissioners. The post is now unfilled (see paragraph 13).

Down the hall, Mike Mullin is leaving as county attorney after 20 years in office. Mullin is retiring by his accord to pursue private interests. His tenure has been considered exemplary, and his departure has nothing to do with the timing of Mahaney's exit.

Nonetheless, another influential position has been vacated. The housecleaning has reached to other county departments. The former county engineer has been replaced. There is a new county clerk, John Crawford, as well as two new commissioners -- all after recent elections.

The face of county government has been reconstructed with a fresh, new look. Maybe it was coincidental, or maybe it was the wish of the people. Either way, it has implications for all of us.

The county oversees a $100 million budget, and is one of largest employers here. It is a big industry that has gotten much bigger. That is a concern.

You wonder whether previous county officials have ever seen a tax they did not like. County officials instituted a nuisance five-cent gas tax, and then rescinded it. They failed to fully roll back the property-tax rate this year, despite an explosion in new revenues from the emergence of subdivisions and major retailers within the county.

It is a matter of a bloated county government becoming more bloated. Yeah, the additional tax revenues helped balance the county budget and sugarcoat a rather bleak financial condition. (This improvement was attributed to Mahaney's guidance.) But a surge in tax revenues will improve any budget.

The unresolved tendency is still to spend, however, and borrow money to pay off old debts. With the new blood, hopefully this will change.

Between the high tax rate here and soaring property assessments, the county's growth could be choked off like a hangman in a noose. It gets worse when you consider the exorbitant insurance costs for residents and businesses alike due to our proximity to the coast.

Whose property insurance did not increase in cost this year -- even though our area has fortunately been spared for 40 years from any catastrophic hurricanes? It is part of a disturbing trend in Florida.

Go to the local coffee shop and listen. Taxes and insurance are sure to get their share of the conversations. Especially if someone owns a business or investment property.

The displeasure of residents with local government here is obvious. Just read the letters to the editor in your local paper, pleading for an answer. Even with the recent changes, the county is still mired in chaos, having to find another county administrator.

If in some way this is a commentary on the displeasure of residents about the county government, it is coming in loud and clear. The caveat is that sometimes you must be careful what you wish for -- it may not be what it seems.

The grass may not be greener on the other side. It may simply be seeded with temporary rye that dies off in the spring.

Regardless, let's nourish a new crop of personnel, and cherish what is hopefully a cleaner and more-efficient governmental house.

Sobering Story of Austerity /September 2011

John Crawford is heading out on a road show with sobering news for any politicians who are still punch-drunk on spending.

Government -- at all levels -- will experience "shrinking tax revenues for some time to come," he says.

Crawford is qualified with such opinions. He is the clerk of circuit courts and the comptroller for Nassau County. As part of his duties, he oversees the county's finances, including some $60 million set aside for capital projects and reserves.

Others should heed Crawford's message. He'll tell his story of austerity to anyone who'll listen -- citizens, organizations, and, of course, political leaders.

He's not trying to be sensational or dramatic. He believes with the conviction of a judge that property values in the state are not going to rebound anytime soon. This would mean the primary driver of tax receipts for Florida municipalities will continue along a long-term detour.

As property values decline because of a surplus of foreclosures and short sales in Florida, fewer taxes are generated -- unless political leaders hike tax rates. Otherwise, government spending must continue to be curtailed. Instead of music to their ears, this is a depressing message that most politicians don't want to hear on local or state levels.

"It's not over -- it's just beginning," says Crawford about declining tax receipts. "And politicians are in denial. They don't get it ... from the courthouse to the White House."

So Crawford has assumed a role of messenger and hit the streets to deliver the news -- whether county commissioners or others like it or not. "I'm going to put it out in the public's view," Crawford says.

Crawford shows a color-coded map of Florida that details delinquent or foreclosed mortgages by county. In Nassau County, more than 10 percent of mortgages are in trouble as of June.

In neighboring Duval County, the rate is slightly lower. But in South Florida, the delinquencies of at least 90 days range from 15 to 25 percent. This backlog will inevitably impact existing valuations, since distressed properties mostly sell at discounted prices.

"We're fixing to get inundated (with foreclosures)," Crawford says. "We've always felt immune in Nassau County." This will also impact state revenues. This past year, Florida legislators have to plug a $3 billion budget shortfall. Next year will be as bad, or worse.

Within the county, some government bodies are raising tax rates to circumvent the declining property values. In Fernandina Beach, city commissioners even went out and borrowed $5.6 million for new projects.

Crawford winces at the thought of frivolous and irrational spending. He has urged county commissioners here to avoid such temptations, even with interest rates at historic lows.

"Here's our neighbor ... borrowing money," Crawford says. "I worry about it infecting our county commissioners."

Nassau County has compiled a sufficient safety net of reserves. But with $67 million in debt and another $30 million required to service these obligations, Crawford is urging commissioners to shun debt and follow a path of frugality. (County departments have reduced spending by as much as 10 percent each of the past few years.)

"All of the assumptions we've been able to rely on are all changing," Crawford says. "Our needs are met. We didn't come here today on a dirt road."

Hopefully, the road leading from here will be one of prosperity.

Political Fireworks Spark Explosion   /February 2007

It is comforting to learn that Nassau County suddenly has so few problems that it can turn its attention toward arresting stargazers on the beach.

A juvenile proposal from a freshman commissioner to close county beaches and parks on Amelia Island at night met as much opposition as a proposal to send more U.S. troops to Iraq. That is, if you define opposition as hundreds of disgruntled residents taking time on a weekday evening to cram the county commission chambers in protest.

Or if you define opposition as an e-mail campaign that flooded commissioners' computers in vehement dissent.

It was apparently perceived as more than closing beaches and parks after dark. It was taking away a freedom. The new law would have impacted well-traveled Peter's Point Park and the new, much-used boat ramp on the north end of the island (as well as the American Beach access and park).

You might have thought a new, bright-eyed and idealistic commissioner would tackle one of a myriad of issues in an inaugural campaign. There are plenty of issues here to address.

A mountain of debt approaching $100 million. Uncontrolled growth. Crowded and bumpy roadways. A lack of a cohesive building code and tree ordinance. Instability within many county departments. Steadily rising taxes. A crisis in obtaining homeowners' insurance. Small businesses on financial respirators.

A still-inferior financial rating for the county. Some $1 million dollars of county funds -- stolen by an unsupervised supervisor -- yet to be recouped. Unresolved repairs on a $30 million courthouse project. A landfill that is filling up. And a general displeasure with prior county commissions.

If it sounds like a soap opera, that's because it is. And county officials have a starring role in it. So when the attention turned to curbing vandalism and antics at county parks and beaches by closing them at night, it took many residents by surprise. In simple terms, you have got to be kidding.

The proposal, dressed up as what would become a new law, died a quick death. It summoned unimaginable numbers and types of residents. The sponsoring commissioner never anticipated it either, judging from his backpedaling, deer-in-the-headlights reaction.

A new cabinet of political officials has been mandated in many ways -- and greeted with guarded optimism. This is not a good start. An excess gas tax has been repealed under the new regime, and the county administrator ousted.

Maybe the latter was necessary to begin heading in a new direction. Or maybe it was a matter of new officials keeping their promises with constituents. Either way, this should not have been the sequel.

What will we do for an encore? Ban joggers and bicyclists from county roadways? Levy a fine against anyone collecting shells and sharks' teeth on the beaches? How about requiring all beachgoers to purchase a beach badge?

No reason to stop with trying to restrict beach activities at night. The proposal was well-researched and thought out, however. It contained a clause lifting the beach ban for at least the Fourth of July -- until 10 p.m. or something silly.

This would interfere with some of the annual, much-anticipated fireworks. For hundreds of residents, these are preferable over political fireworks.

Learning from a Neighbor /April 2007

Sometimes, you don't have to reinvent the wheel. Just take the wheel you have, and rebalance it with new ideas.

The issues we face in Nassau County can be overwhelming. Accommodating growth while protecting the environment. Figuring how to house the new residents, build schools and provide services, and put in roads to transport them. And not trample the rights and lifestyles of existing residents.

However, we're not the first county to experience explosive growth. It's going on all around us. We can learn from our neighbors. Create a citizen's task force with purpose and meaning -- and assign it to visit and study effectively run counties. You know, to observe what they are doing. Steal a few good ideas.

Take Charlotte County in southwest Florida, for instance. Like here, Charlotte has lots of water and marshes and parks. It's twice the size of Nassau County, with a population that has doubled every 10 years. It is trying to balance growth while protecting its small and pristine area, tucked away on its Gulf cove between Sarasota and Fort Myers.

Charlotte County has won plenty of awards, so it must be doing something right. It's been hailed for years as one of the best places to live in America by Money magazine; Golf Digest recognized it as one of the best golf areas; its main city, Punta Gorda, was called the "Best Small Place for Business and Career" by Forbes magazine; and Kiplinger's and Florida Trend magazines have praised it.

So the place has appeal and a dynamite resume. It also has a landfill that earned a prestigious national award, with a lifespan of another 20 years. Charlotte doesn't mess with much of a city-owned or county-owned marina, but has plenty of private ones, offering boat rentals and fishing charters and sightseeing cruises.

It also boasts the Charlotte Harbor, with 50 kayak and canoe trails and a plethora of canals. Most of the harbor is preserved land. It is fed by the Peace and Myakka rivers, forming one of the largest estuaries in the state. And the Babcock/Webb wildlife area encompasses 79,000 acres of undisturbed pines.

15

The county carries some debt on its balance sheet, but it is a drop in a financial bucket compared with its revenues. It has a thorough, 229-page report available for public viewing. The "Comprehensive Annual Financial Report" spells out its expenses and its income in plain, easy-to-read tables. Talk about financial visibility. And its numbers check out, verified in an audit by Ernst & Young.

The county has a solid financial rating. It even has the resources and resiliency to respond to a direct hit from Hurricane Charley a couple of years ago. Its departments collaborated to quickly rebuild. Its waste department collected two million yards of debris. More than 46,000 street signs had to be replaced.

With Charlotte County's increased population, it must handle more waste. Its single, state-of-the-art landfill uses a compactor to reduce the size of its wastes, while converting yard trash (leaves, sticks, etc.) into mulch that it offers for free to residents.

The county recycles tires and appliances and batteries. It uses several innovative waste-handling techniques, such as alternating cover soils (over the garbage) to conserve space. The county did not reinvent the waste-handling wheel, however. It contracts with a private company, SCS Engineers, which specializes in complex landfill issues and conservation.

The county constantly protects its estuaries and marshes, and improves its public facilities. It just invested $2.7 million to improve one of its beaches. It constructed pavilions, a restroom/shower facility, and a 1,000-foot-long boardwalk.

And there is much more that Charlotte County is doing right. It makes for good reading. Now we just need someone here to read it.

Natives Are Getting Restless   /September 2011

The natives appear restless within Fernandina Beach.

Drumbeats of change echo through the distance -- sounding a new direction for the city. Residents gather in private pockets and in public forums to voice concerns and coordinate efforts. They are aiming spears of protest toward the spheres of influence here.

A pattern of confusing missteps and misjudgments by city officials has ruffled residents. Relentless tax and fee increases. Unchecked borrowing and spending. Trivial projects. And an air of arrogance instilled in their decisions.

If there was a town crier in Fernandina Beach, an old-style messenger and broadcaster of events, he might be crying right now. Or maybe laughing. Not with amusement, but with a heckle of contempt.

"You can't make up this stuff," says Charlie Corbett, a long-time resident and quick-quipping activist who has shepherded the public outcry.

Corbett, who is retired, makes it his job to scour City Hall for data on actions and issues -- and to disseminate it. He attends meetings, confronts officials, and plainly cares for the city.

He recites the most glaring blunders and shortcomings of city officials, almost by rote. He summarizes their actions as the "epitome of ridiculous-ity." So here he goes:

■ The city's whimsical and tyrannical use of impact fees has infuriated residents, so they've risen up through a class-action lawsuit. Recently, city officials secretly tried to assess nearly $800,000 of impact fees against local restaurants -- and make it appear as though the state initiated it.

■ A long-standing lawsuit between the airport operator and the city endured a new twist. Current officials have now taken ownership of it, appealing the latest $1 million verdict against the city. Another fruitless appeal will cost thousands more in attorney's fees.

■ Commissioners extended their terms by seven months when they moved the city election date from April to November (when most other elections are held). The city will realize some

$14,000 in savings by holding the city elections in November -- that is, when another election is scheduled. There is no other election this fall, and therefore no savings. "That's still my favorite," says Corbett.

■ City commissioners recently approved borrowing up to $5.6 million for downtown projects that few residents apparently want. Instead of letting voters decide whether to indebt the city during a difficult economic period, officials acted on their own.

The interest on the borrowed funds will be paid through an assessment on residents' utility bills. One commissioner expressed concerns that people may think "we're pulling something over on them." According to Corbett, "Yeah, that's exactly what we think."

■ Paradoxically, the two major projects underlying the $5.6 million loan involve buildings that the city does not yet own -- the old post office and the old First Union building on Centre Street. Opening Alachua Street at the waterfront and erecting a waterfront park are two other projects that hardly exhibit any urgency.

■ The city manager continues to push ahead with several unpopular projects: installing parking kiosks and moving the boardwalk at Main Beach. He's doing it under the guise of searching for "new revenues."

■ The idyllic, twinkling tree lights in downtown have been removed and replaced with dim ground lights. Again, it is another misstep by city officials who don't seem to be willing to revisit it.

■ The city increased its property tax rate again -- by more than the state allows without a super majority vote. Ironically, several of the current commissioners were elected on an anti-tax platform.

■ City building officials have been allowed to run roughshod over local construction projects, even though there are a precious few in a weak economy. Excessive fines, fees and harassment have been hallmarks of city action.

The list is longer than there is space here. The mayor reportedly doesn't understand why everyone is angry. Hopefully the mayor will read this column.

Making Greenway Green Again /March 2007

A much-anticipated study has been completed on the Egan's Creek Greenway -- and how part of it has become a "gray way" from the deaths of acres of trees.

An engineering group used by the Florida Department of Transportation issued the report. The report seems somewhat defensive and vague in nature, since it is pretty much written by the same FDOT affiliates who did the work to create the greenway.

Conservation groups are pouring over every point of the study, and a public hearing will be held to discuss it. Fernandina Beach city commissioners will ultimately decide on how to respond to the findings -- and remedy the deaths of about 50 acres of trees south of Jasmine Street along the greenway.

As a public service, we'll do our best to help interpret the arcane language in the document. The style of the language is somewhere between an encyclopedia and a legal brief. Here are some excerpts, and what they mean in normal words.

■ The document describes: "vegetation changes south of Jasmine Street." The translation is: "some 50 acres of gray, dying red-maple trees."

■ The document asks whether to: "promote saltwater vegetation south of Jasmine Street." The translation is: "Should we mow down another 50 acres of dead trees to cover up a miscalculation?"

■ The document uses thesaurus-enriched terms such as "tide propagation" and "attenuation" and "subconsultants." The implied translation is: The use of confusing terms can leave everyone guessing.

■ The document cites: "clearing of freshwater vegetation -- estimated at $375,000 -- would not be necessary for successful salt marsh restoration." The translation is: "The trees are already dead (south of Jasmine), so let's leave them there in salt water ... otherwise, it'll cost a bunch to clear them."

■ The document cites: "The long-term costs of maintaining the area south of Jasmine Street as a freshwater system should realistically include replanting every 50 years ... the cost is $593,000 for 50 acres." The translation is: "Hey, what's dead is gone, so let's move on ... or else this is really going to be costly for someone (and that someone is not the FDOT)."

■   The document cites: "If a tide barrier is installed on the south side of Jasmine Street ... the cost exceeds $2 million." The translation is: "This is the best way to correct the saltwater intrusion south of Jasmine Street -- and it's expensive." A question looms, however: Why was it not done from the beginning?

The greenway project began with FDOT installing a new tide gate at Atlantic Avenue. This now allows saltwater to flow from Egan's Creek into the expanse between Atlantic Avenue and Jasmine Street -- the proposed "greenway."

The FDOT was involved because it needed to mitigate some saltwater marsh it eradicated in Jacksonville from building a bridge. It therefore took on the project to transform the Egan's Creek Greenway to an original salt marsh.

Now, the saltwater is intruding farther down Egan's Creek, flowing under Jasmine Street and into the forest south of it. This is where the trees are dying. The FDOT study was conducted to determine how to correct the problem.

Environmental groups contend the FDOT should pay for the trees that have died south of Jasmine Street, based upon the city's tree ordinance. The FDOT seems to be taking little responsibility for the unintended tree damage, however, if we are reading the report correctly (not an easy task).

The options appear to be allowing the gray way to "propagate" in their terms across Jasmine Street, or else spending a bunch of money to reverse the massacre of red maples.

The tree is now in the city's court.

A New Year of Hope /January 2007

A new year. A new beginning. A time for hope, and optimism.

It is also a time to review what happened last year, and to plan for this year. If we could create a wish list, here are 10 developments that would certainly benefit our community.

1- Rectify the county landfill mess. This conundrum is becoming more complicated with each load of trash. Privatizing the landfill is probably a good thing, but most companies would not assume the debt that comes with it. Either way, the landfill is filling up, and the debt (from closing old landfills and opening this one) is costing taxpayers each day.

2- Continue improving the look and functionality of the Fernandina Beach marina. A marina is a prized jewel of any waterside community. It is a conduit to a steady flow of business and tourism. It also can complement industries such as fishing and boating.

3- Address the roads here to accommodate the impending growth. Nothing is worse than traffic-snarled roadways. If anyone has not noticed, the traffic here is getting worse. It is too late for esoteric planning measures -- something must be done, and fast. Call in state, regional, and local forces to make it happen.

4- Control and manage growth. Fighting the growth here is unrealistic. Making it conform to high standards has been done elsewhere. It can be done here. It takes planning, vision, and the willingness to enforce codes.

5- Devise fair and equitable tax codes. There is plenty of land and properties within the county to share the tax burden. There seems to be inequalities between similar types of properties within the county.

6- Bring relief to small, locally owned businesses. Owners of businesses and investment properties are getting squeezed between higher taxes and rising insurance costs. Local officials must address this, or else the small business owner will become extinct. This is especially true in the county seat of Fernandina Beach, where the business climate is being threatened by new retail centers elsewhere in the county.

21

7- Tighten up the county budget. County officials must consider rolling back the tax rate, like numerous other local boards have done. If the county cannot roll back its tax rate during this phenomenal surge in growth -- and in additional taxes -- when can it?

8- Figure a mutually agreeable density for downtown Fernandina Beach. This is a touchy subject, but cooler heads should allow for a compromise in density. This would appease both environmentalists and business owners.

9- Bring continuity to the planning and zoning departments in both Fernandina Beach and in the county. This has been a difficult task, with the revolving door of personnel in these areas. The demand is extreme on these departments, and their roles are important.

10- Enact county ordinances for consistent design of new construction -- and to protect trees. You don't have to be a tree hugger to notice the difference between the Amelia Island Parkway and State Highway A1A in Yulee. One pivotal word: trees. And innovative designs.

These are idealistic developments -- of hope. And if realized, ones of joy.

A Dubious Distinction   /October 2011

Fernandina Beach has earned another distinction that places it within the top five percent of the cities in Florida.

Of all the cities in the state, only five percent (or one out of 20) raised its property tax rate this year and also borrowed a significant amount of money. This is according to the Florida League of Cities, which tracks this sort of thing.

This is a dubious distinction. Maybe Fernandina Beach officials know something that other city officials don't, or maybe not. Either way, local officials are following a tax-and-spend, borrow-and-spend approach.

As a justification, some local commissioners have cited the internal investment of $80 million that the Omni Amelia Island Plantation will make into its property. This is indeed an investment (new hotel rooms, a new ballroom, etc.) because it will provide an anticipated return -- by creating additional revenues streams.

Fernandina Beach commissioners raised the property tax rate because it will generate about the same amount of revenues as prior years (as property values have fallen). While families and businesses are cutting back and doing more with less, city officials felt entitled to hold the line.

In addition, new projects costing more than $5 million and as much as $15 million in borrowed money will produce virtually no tax revenues (these are a revitalized post office building, a new library, a new waterfront park, opening Alachua Street, and improving the crossings at Front Street).

This is a major difference between what the Omni is doing and what city officials are planning. And, by the way, the city is borrowing its money through taxes and levies on the public; the Omni is using private funds.

Meanwhile, city officials point out that borrowing costs are low right now, and that they are seizing this opportunity to borrow. This is like a family receiving a credit card offer in the mail to borrow $100,000 at a very low rate. A responsible family throws this offer in the trash, not because the rate is unattractive -- but because you have to pay the money back, with interest.

Government officials on the national level on down to the local level are not grasping this concept right now. Borrowing money feels good at the time, but not during the 30 years it takes to pay it back.

Omni Amelia Island Plantation is investing internally into projects that will improve the resort -- and generate additional revenues. The Ritz Carlton, Amelia Island has expanded its conference rooms to accommodate larger meetings and the likes. It also helps drive revenues.

In other cities, St. Augustine added a community theater that attracts major musical acts and fosters tax-generating activities. Here, the Yulee International Trade Plex and the Ritz-Carlton both are additions that have substantially improved our quality of life and our tax base. It can be done again here, even with public funds -- but the city plan is just not the answer.

A major civic and political leader on the west side of Nassau County says he can't wait to get his News-Leader each week. He likes to keep up with what Fernandina Beach city officials are doing. And laugh.

"Fernandina Beach is the laughing stock of the county," he says, referring to the recent decisions and antics by city officials.

Unfortunately, this kind of entertainment doesn't generate any additional revenues for the city.

Getting House in Order   /February 2007

The county is getting its financial house in order.

A recent upgrade in its financial rating is testimony to this. The county's financial rating determines the interest rate at which it can borrow money, for instance.

However, the financial house still requires some straightening and cleaning. You see, the inflow of new taxes from the explosion of development here could make any budget look better.

The assessed value of properties in Nassau County has doubled in recent years. This generates more tax revenues, especially since county officials neglected to roll back the tax rate this year.

With each new shopping center the size of Wal-Mart, another $200,000 or more in new taxes is generated every year. If you look around, there is enough new construction to fund the county's budget for years.

The county not only failed to roll back its tax rate -- to compensate for higher valuations and new development -- it also increased the landfill fees, and assessed an offensive 5-cents-per-gallon tax on each gallon of gas sold here.

Due to public outcry, the gas tax (which is in addition to plenty of other taxes on gas) has been repealed -- as of next year, that is. So the county has essentially raised property taxes, increased landfill fees, and placed a rarely used tax on gas.

Little has been done to pare back spending, or to control the size of local government, or solve other financial conundrums. The budget just keeps growing, and growing.

It's just not as noticeable right now from the outside – like a house undergoing interior repairs.

Protect Our Trees, Please   /July 2008

It is Nassau County's trademark. Locals cherish it. Visitors covet it.

It is the natural beauty of our area -- from the rivers to the marshes to the ocean. The centerpiece of the beauty is not just our waterways, but also our bountiful trees. Few coastal areas can boast such an array of towering trees.

However, the natural beauty is under assault from reckless development. Look no farther than the hodgepodge of construction along the A1A corridor in Yulee, or the clear-cutting of lots around the county.

In a preventative and protective measure, Nassau County officials are finally crafting uniform guidelines for such development. And at the root of the measure is the protection of the most precious resource -- our trees.

County officials will take up the new development codes at their Jan. 14 and 28 meetings. They will seek public input at both meetings before voting on the measures as they now stand, or as revised.

The new measures are vast, and call for the protection of native tree canopies; the requirement of buffers along wetlands; and the enactment of landscaping standards for new construction. The provisions would only impact the unincorporated areas of the county. Local cities have their own codes.

Some locals contend that the county had agreed on uniform codes for development along A1A at the time the Lofton Square retail center was constructed. A tasteful buffer of trees fronts the center on A1A, and a sidewalk also borders the roadway.

Things apparently changed after that. The big-box retailers reportedly had little interest in following such specific directives. The result is what we now have -- a clear-cutting of trees with orchards of skimpy, hand-me-down replacements, and bordering gargantuan parking lots.

For the most part, local developers are responsible and interested in preserving our natural assets. They live here and have reputations to uphold. Those from out of town hardly have such vested interests.

It is imperative that the public voices its opinion. Local officials took notice when 300 angry citizens turned out to oppose closing the county beaches and parks after sunset. Officials listened when a vociferous group opposed a new apartment complex in Yulee.

This is not about hugging trees. This is about requiring responsible development -- and being able to enforce it. You can be assured that those associated with the development profession will attend, as is their right.

The final codes should be fair and equitable, but should contain enough teeth to put a bite in shoddy development. The new commercial centers and developments on the drawing board are backed by big money.

They have big-time attorneys who handle such issues all day, every day. But the public might cannot be underestimated.

You might ask how the county handled new construction in the past, if such specific and accountable measures were not in place. Look out your window when driving down A1A next time.

The results are obvious.

County Tries New Exercise   /May 2007

Exercise is recommended to maintain a healthy lifestyle. It is useful in trimming fat and maintaining a strong heart.

A new exercise being used by county officials is also targeted at cutting fat -- within our local government, that is. In a praiseworthy exercise, county officials are scrutinizing their budgets for excess fat and surpluses.

This exercise in frugality and efficiency is necessary, due to a possible reduction in tax revenues. State lawmakers are still considering a mandate on lower tax rates, which would in turn reduce revenues for counties and cities. Local officials would essentially have to learn to live on low-fat, or in this case, low-tax diets.

So officials are reviewing expenses. In itself, this is a positive exercise, even though it is being done in response to a possible state mandate.

County and city officials should regularly review their budgets. Otherwise, new expenditures are added each year, on top of those from the prior year. In this way, a budget continues to grow, and grow.

One county official had probably the best idea in years. Commissioner Barry Holloway proposed adopting a strategy of "zero-based budgeting." This is a practice whereby each department must justify its expenses -- from the prior year as well as proposed increases for the next year.

It is not a situation whereby previous expenditures are grand-fathered in -- since they were paid the year before. The county has not tried this type of fat-burning exercise in the past. It has always employed a "wish list" methodology, whereby county officials would submit budgets that included items they could ideally use. These are items they would like to have, but not need.

The tax revenues would be allocated and granted based upon this "wish list" approach. This is part of the reason that county officials have failed to roll back the tax rate in recent years, despite a surplus of revenues. There are always new items on which to spend new money.

Like with any type of exercise, some county officials are begrudgingly taking part. They feel the state is essentially victimizing them by forcing a reduction in their budget, and thus endangering pet projects. Some even carpooled to Tallahassee to voice their opposition to the possible tax cuts.

We did not see a caravan of residents parading to the state capital to oppose the tax cuts, however. Instead, there has been an ear-piercing cacophony of pleas for lower taxes.

Local officials have threatened to reduce vital services such as police and fire protection if backed into a corner by state lawmakers. These services are called "vital" for a reason -- because they are important. There are plenty of extras that could be paired back before impacting vital services.

For one, some county officials have reportedly hired personal attorneys to represent them in case of lawsuits. This sounds more like a luxury than a necessity (we do have a county attorney, after all).

And this does not mean that county employees will suffer. Most of the increases in the county budget have gone elsewhere -- and not in employees' pockets. Most employees received modest pay raises last year.

The largest pay increases went to the former administrator and the former attorney. The operative word is "former," since neither is still employed by the county. There are obviously plenty of entries that could be reduced from a new and improved "low-tax" diet.

This is, after all, the heart of the matter.

Where Has Money Gone?   /June 2007

Lower property taxes could soon be coming to a neighborhood near you.

That is if state lawmakers get their way – and local officials do not.

In a dubious effort, several Nassau County commissioners have paraded against state proposals to force down property taxes in much of the state. It seems some local commissioners do not want to give residents a break on the vice-grip of escalating taxes.

In the last seven years, property-tax revenues in Nassau County have increased by 50 to 70 percent – depending on the source of information. Other estimates indicate tax revenues have nearly doubled during that time, due in large part to soaring property values.

Meanwhile, the county population has grown slightly. The latest census reveals 64,000 residents in Nassau County, a modest increase – but hardly in pace with the additional tax revenues. So where has the money gone? That's a multi-million-dollar question.

-- To pay down county debt? Hardly. The county's long-term debt has been skyrocketing in recent years. In fact, the county has regularly overspent its budget each year, and had to dip into the coming year's reserves to fund operations.

-- To fund additional county services? It's hard to see an increase of 50 to 100 percent in services being rendered.

-- To add additional staff? Somewhat. Several county officials have hired individual legal counsel for themselves, for instance. It leaves you wondering what the county attorney's duties are. But it's difficult to see new employees costing millions of dollars.

-- To build additional stuff? Yes, when you consider a $32 million courthouse annex that was funded mostly by borrowed money. The interest on such debt can cost millions of dollars a year.

In the meantime, state legislators are pushing for reduced property taxes around the state. They realize the property-tax burden will eventually cause the state's economy to crumble. Anticipated revenues from real-estate activity have declined so significantly in Florida this year that state officials have had to dip into reserves for operations.

Real-estate activity has driven the state's economy for years, in addition to revenues from tourism. Spiraling taxes will inevitably impede real-estate transactions.

Local officials do not share this foresight. They only see a need for additional revenues to pay for their pet projects – and a continuation of uncontrolled spending.

The tax revenues received by the county commission here this year will exceed $50 million. Another $50 million will go to public schools.

The school board has exercised fiscal control, however. In fact, the school board built the new Yulee High School with available money from its budget and from the state, incurring little or no debt. This is clearly an example of a frugal use of public tax dollars.

The county can learn from this. In response to a habit of lavish spending, County Clerk John Crawford has held county commissioners accountable. Crawford has challenged elaborate expenses, urging commissioners to identify available revenues to cover the costs. This is a stark contrast to the borrow-and-spend habits of prior commissions.

Some local officials have spoken harshly about the state's efforts to reduce taxes. They have defended their spending practices, and pleaded that lower tax revenues will force a reduction in vital services such as police protection, road repairs, and even library offerings.

These are the last areas that should be reduced. While cutbacks can be made in any areas, to threaten to pare back vital services is a lame excuse.

A Lexicon of Confusion   /November 2007

Those who attended the county meeting last week on the proposed Nassau Center project endured an ear-popping barrage of an alphabet-soup lexicon that lasted for hours.

It's little wonder why more residents do not attend these land-development meetings. Though the meetings and hearings are of monumental importance, they are about as easy to sit through as multiple root canals.

Terms such as "FLUM" and "concurrency" and "round-trips" and "intensity of land use" and "PUDs" are tossed around like objects in a hurricane. They are enough to make your head spin and your stomach queasy.

The only people who understand such terms are developers and their lawyers, as well as some of the county planning officials. But even those county officials seemed perplexed about the longstanding agreement (it has origins going back 20 years) governing the Nassau Center proposal.

The 70-acre Nassau Center has far-reaching implications. It will be positioned along Chester Road at the intersection with Highway A1A in Yulee. The intersection already includes a bank and the side entrance to Home Depot.

In futuristic plans, Chester Road appears in many contexts. It connects current and future thoroughfares and is a hurricane-evacuation route. Locating a major shopping center such as Nassau Center on the corner of Chester Road and A1A could be problematic in many ways.

However, county commissioners sided with the developers' proposal and voted to move ahead with the project. They apparently felt the $100,000 or so that the developer apparently had invested in his plans were reason enough to approve the complex.

In addition, the developer pledged to put in a turning lane off of A1A onto Chester Road as a concession to moving traffic along the crowded corridor.

The commissioners' decision came in the face of objections and concerns from county planning officials. In several instances, planning officials flat out cautioned commissioners about moving ahead with the complex without further study. This is due mostly to the congestion of Chester Road as well as A1A, which already is over-capacity by most measures.

Sometimes you wonder if county commissioners understand the terminology and complexities of such projects. They rely primarily on their own attorney, who is new, as well as their planning and growth-management officials. And the initial sequence for approvals begins with the county planning and zoning board.

When commissioners move directly in the face of opposition from planning officials, you have to wonder about their motives and urgency. However, the county commission has given carte blanche to most developments in the area.

They rarely even require concessions of developers as part of normal give-and-take negotiations over a new shopping complex or subdivision.

Many of the developers are armed with teams of lawyers, who often overwhelm and out-debate local planning officials. They are equipped with guile and expertise -- and they have time to prepare for such hearings.

And most importantly, they can talk the talk.

Even though 2007 is drawing to a close, there are many local issues that have received little resolution.

Since resolutions are a big part of new-year planning, let's review the status of these problematic, open-ended issues. We'll make it a list for ease of planning.

Forest of Death. It seems the so-called "study" phase of resolving the saltwater seepage from the Egan's Creek greenway is taking longer than anticipated. State officials are apparently having difficulty figuring out a way to prevent salt water from traveling under Jasmine Street into the forest south of it. You can identify the area by the gray, dying trees.

Hoover Dam? Not only have state officials waffled on a cure for the saltwater seepage, but they've also spent a ridiculous amount of time and money resolving another short-sighted error. They have spent between $1 million and $2 million resolving erosion caused by the free-flowing waters of Egan's Creek.

As part of the greenway restoration, Egan's Creek has been allowed to flow freely under Atlantic Avenue. A bulkhead originally constructed by state officials along the bank south of Atlantic Avenue nearly fell down, so they've come back with a deluxe concrete barrier that resembles Hoover Dam. Maybe they didn't want to be criticized a second time -- for a second error -- so they went overboard with a new, ridiculously stout bulkhead.

Fernandina Beach Waterfront. Though there have been many hours of efforts already put into redoing the waterfront area at the foot of Centre Street, much work still lies ahead. Current plans include an expanded marina, walkways, parks, and commercial/residential locations. It can be something really special.

A1A Logjam. The congestion and spiraling construction along this pivotal corridor is a pressing issue. Alternative roads and beautification and widening of A1A are all possibilities. The time to put these into action is now.

Unrealistic Property Assessments. Except for homeowners protected by the homestead exemption, all others are getting clobbered by excessive property assessments. These assessments determine how much you are taxed. The over-taxed entities include businesses, investment properties, and commercial locations. A zealous property appraiser is conjuring up taxable valuations that, in the current market, are nowhere near the prices for which properties can sell. It is killing local businesses and investment properties here.

Local Taxes. Tax rates here are coming down in a refreshing move. Most of the reduction is due to a state mandate for local municipalities to cut taxes. Even though this is occurring, many people will not feel the benefit. You see, as part of the tax equation, the tax rate is multiplied by the assessed value of a property to determine your taxes due. With soaring assessments, even lower tax rates will result in little savings for local residents. This will suffocate our local and state economy if not addressed.

County Finances. While there is still work to do, the county has succeeded in improving its financial status. There is still a mountain of long-term debt that has to be overcome, but with Clerk John Crawford questioning expenditures and financial guru Ted Selby making the numbers work, the county's situation has improved.

County Landfill. The landfill's outlook has improved as a sizable debt attached to the landfill has been lifted. Now, the next step is to decide how to operate it the most efficiently and with the most longevity.

Congestion. Though it's nothing compared to urban-sprawl areas such as Atlanta, the traffic congestion here has steadily worsened. It will truly be noticed as tourists continue to gravitate here, especially during the summer.

Open/Green Space. It seems that Fernandina Beach officials have a lot of open space in their possession, and want to keep it that way. It took a hard-fought debate to approve a water slide for the empty, sand-spur-filled lot at Main Beach. Some city officials wanted to preserve their "open/green space," while others saw a mutual benefit in a private/public venture.

The city currently sits on some millions of dollars of vacant properties, which generate no taxes and provide little public benefit (other than providing a place to put a sign).

Since when did the city get into the real estate business, anyhow?

Impress Us with Frugality

Fernandina Beach residents used to watch the city commission meetings here for sheer entertainment.

Years ago, a longtime commissioner would berate unsuspecting speakers at public hearings -- if they displayed a lack of knowledge, or said something he felt was stupid.

Decades ago, commissioners would go to the Palace Saloon after a meeting for a round of beers -- and whatever else it took to settle a disagreement or an issue. It is all part of an illustrious past.

The city, and county, has grown substantially since then. And it's not funny anymore. There is too much on the line. The decisions being made will color our future. This is now serious stuff.

Commissioners at both the city and county levels do not conduct themselves with a wild-west flippancy of their predecessors. They act much more professionally. However, their decisions sometimes border on the humorous.

Today, commissioners are hardly handling growth responsibly -- especially at the county level. Roads are getting crowded without a plan to improve them. Shopping centers are being approved with abandon and then chaotically thrown together.

High taxes are forcing businesses to close and residents to pick up and find shelter in lower-tax places. Meanwhile, commissioners are lavishly spending money by boosting staffs, buying fleets of cars and toys, and constructing unnecessary buildings. We deserve, and should expect, better.

In recollecting some big-ticket purchases of the past, which may or may not have been the best use of money, consider these:

■ The county spent $32 million for a new courthouse annex (and jail, which the county had to build), although the funds were not there. The county borrowed the money and has paid a substantial cost for it. Each year the interest and principal due on the loan: about $2.2 million.

■ The county opted to buy a new emergency radio system. Emergency workers needed a new system to communicate, but the system came with a big price tag -- about $8 million. Some felt there were cheaper alternatives.

■　　The city has already used most of the $5 million it has recently borrowed to improve the marina. The results of the work may not be so visible to the eye, since some of it went to infrastructure repairs. It just seems that the money has been used rather quickly.

■　　The city opted to hire additional employees this year, at the opposition of at least Commissioner Joe Gerrity. Times will be tougher as a likely recession works its way through our economy and state-mandated tax cuts are assimilated. The city is no longer the employment agency for the area -- a posture it has adopted for too many years.

Some of the commissioners now in office had little to do with the above-referenced decisions. These were not necessarily bad decisions, although they each were pricey.

Those are water under the bridge anyhow. The future is now. Entertain us from here with sound decisions -- and impeccable logic and frugality.

A Circus without Laughter   /July 2007

The developments surrounding Egan's Creek have become somewhat of a circus. The only thing missing is a high-top tent – but there are plenty of clowns.

There has been a circus-like ring of activity. First of all, millions of state dollars were spent on a project to retool the valves under Atlantic Avenue and allow the saltwater of Egan's Creek to flow freely into the marsh south of there.

A few years later, another million dollars or so (of state money) are being spent on refurbishing a protective wall constructed along a river bank south of Atlantic Avenue. Installed improperly, the wall was being pushed away by the renewed flow of water.

The rushing tides were also washing away the land behind the wall, endangering a property there. At least state officials are righting a wrong. A million dollars is a steep price to pay, however.

Nearby, the Egan's Creek recreational park was replanted with grass after underground refurbishments. Youth baseball and football teams frequently practice at the popular park. That will not be happening for a while, however.

A large pile of rocks now occupies much of the park. Apparently, the rocks will be placed along Egan's Creek. However, grass cannot grow if it is covered by rocks.

In a related act, the saltwater freely flowing through Egan's Creek continues to kill trees south of Jasmine Street. In an oversight, state officials did not believe the saltwater would travel through small pipes under Jasmine and intrude into a wooded area south of there.

Houses border what is now a gray, ghostly forest. State officials are studying a cure for the leakage under Jasmine Street. But it may take time. Meanwhile, trees continue to die, encroaching on the houses south of Jasmine Street.

In yet another circus act, the former owner of property south of Jasmine now wants it back -- or else he wants the city to pay him for it. Smiley Lee gifted the property to the city, with certain conditions.

He has publicly announced his frustration with the current condition of the property south of Jasmine Street, and sent a letter to the city with his new stipulations. There has been no resolution.

But this circus still has more acts. There are reports that there used to be public dumps (you know, where you throw away old appliances and garbage and the likes) along Jasmine Street, where the saltwater is flowing and permeating the soil.

You see, for decades the saltwater of Egan's Creek was blocked by sealed valves at Atlantic Avenue, and was unable to enter the marsh south of Atlantic -- or seep under Jasmine Street. There was only fresh water in these parts.

Farther up the creek, a hotel is proposed for a site along Sadler Road. It is where Egan's Creek crosses under Sadler and continues to Simmons Road.

Opponents of the hotel contend animals use this corridor to migrate around the island. They say the hotel would impede the animals' movements. And you need animals to complete a circus.

You know, any circus must come to a climactic close. And when it does, hopefully there will not be any Harry Potter-like sequels. One showing is enough.

Strikes ... and Base Hits   /August 2007

Strikes are good in bowling, but bad in baseball -- especially when there are three of them.

Here is a local case of when three strikes are good, however.

County commissioners have struck out lately on several initiatives that are lending credence to a new start, and a new way of thinking. In the past, county officials have been maligned for uncontrolled spending and imprudent decisions.

They have progressed in three noticeable areas:

-- County officials have voted to erase a pesky $100 annual landfill fee for taxpayers and also moved toward a big-picture answer on handling the landfill.

Local officials will seek the guidance of an outside landfill company to address what has been a money-gulping operation. A huge debt engulfing the landfill has been paid off recently with excess funds.

The county now believes an outside company may be interested in operating a solvent landfill, or at least advising on it. To make ends meet, the county had been accepting garbage from several other counties to increase its revenues.

This imprudent practice put the local landfill in a dubious position of filling up sooner rather than later. (You would then have to build another landfill, or pay to have your garbage taken elsewhere.)

-- In a second positive action, county officials appear to be obeying a state mandate to reduce taxes. They have proposed a budget for next year that includes reasonable tax cuts handed down by state legislators.

By the way local officials initially reacted to the required tax cuts, it appeared they might try to vote their way out of the measures. Local taxing agencies can use a super-majority vote to override a part of the state mandate. This does not appear to be the case. County officials are proposing to reduce the tax rate by more than 10 percent next year.

-- Last, by not least, the county appears to be headed toward filling the unoccupied seat of county administrator, or coordinator.

The most optimistic development here is that acting administrator, Ted Selby, has thrown his hat into a less-than-crowded ring. Selby, the former county finance director, is obviously a financially versed candidate. Who better than a financial person to oversee a budget of more than $100 million?

The lack of financial acumen got the county into its difficult position in the first place. Selby understands budgets and has guided county officials to comply with the tax reductions. With Selby's direction, it seemed the budget-cutting procedure went smoothly.

Selby also seems to understand that all prior misdeeds are not corrected by simply raising taxes. Higher taxes will usually choke an economy, no matter how strong it appears.

Some of his predecessors never saw a tax they didn't like. Reducing what is spent is a much surer way of improving financial operations gone awry.

Positive developments deserve positive reinforcement. This is a stark improvement from our past. We may begin to like this new direction.

Wow, Take a Bow /October 2007

Stand up. Take a bow. Nassau County officials deserve kudos for this one.

In a deft and insightful move, oft-maligned local officials are paying off the remaining $12.3 million of debt on the county landfill. It could be the first move to tidy up what have been a financial albatross -- and a complete mess.

And they are not borrowing new money to pay the debt, or taking it from another department that might eventually suffer from a loss of funding. They have creatively assembled a pot of money from various sources.

The landfill has been saddled with problems. It is a culmination of prior miscalculations and oversights. Without taking a new direction, it is conceivable that the existing landfill would fill up and become obsolete -- and millions of dollars of remaining debt would have to be carried over to a new landfill (this is what happened with old landfills here).

With innovative financing and delays of new projects, there is money to pay off the $12.3 million debt. Most of it will come from collections of the one-cent sales tax. Here is a breakdown of where it will come from:

-- $3.3 million in revenues and reserve funds from the one-cent sales tax

-- $4.2 million from general fund reserves

-- $4.8 million from the landfill account, including reserves and the $1.7 million payment (for principal and interest this year on the $12.3 million loan).

On one hand, it is reflective of the county's improved financial condition to be able to satisfy the large landfill loan in one swoop. The county is truly flush with cash, due to the growth our area is experiencing. And boosting reserves for rainy days as well as paying off long-term debt are by-products of the financial improvements.

Now, county officials led by County Clerk John Crawford believe they can entice a buyer for the debt-free landfill or a company to manage it. In other parts of the state, this has worked better than with individual counties managing their own landfills.

Using the money to pay off the landfill debt will cause several projects to be delayed, including the new sheriff's office. But county officials are responsibly clearing up one debt before starting others. This is a refreshing change.

Unleash the Bubbly   /July 2007

Uncork the champagne, and revel in the refreshing bubbles of tax relief.

Though difficult to decipher, the mandate handed down by Florida legislators last week is reportedly the largest property-tax cut in our state's history. The mandate affords some $30 billion in property-tax relief to residents and businesses over the next five years.

The new tax cuts are far-reaching. They call for a rollback of property-tax rates to year-ago levels, and limit future tax increases. A special vote by residents is also planned for January to potentially increase and expand the tax exemption of homesteaded properties.

There are some party-pooper types that could take the tax cuts away from us, however. They are your local city and county commissioners. With a swift, near-majority vote, they could crash the party and resurrect the high property taxes hindering our local and state economy.

The most vocal board against the tax cuts has been the Nassau County Commission. This is probably where the biggest threat to tax salvation lies.

County commissioners campaigned against the tax cuts. It is logical to assume these commissioners would still be opposed to them, since they are now law. Several enterprising commissioners took the opportunity to speak out against the tax cuts in a public forum.

Rightfully so, we might add. The county has the most to lose in the state's tax-cut package, since the city and county commissions in the state that have levied the most taxes must now give the most back -- to the people, that is.

While Fernandina Beach city commissioners and local town officials here have been mindful of tax increases, county commissioners have not. Even last year, when tax revenues were overflowing, the county did not fully roll back its property-tax rate.

Under the new laws, an irresponsible commission would not only have to roll back its tax rate to last year's level -- but that rate must then be decreased by as much as another 9 percent. The reductions are based upon how frugal a particular commission has been in handling taxes over the last five years.

The tax package is as confusing as it is sweeping. Several reports of the tax cuts from notable newspapers such as the Tallahassee Democrat and the Miami Herald varied considerably. It was almost like you were reading reports of completely separate legislative action.

Confusion can lead to voter apathy and indecision. An apathetic public might allow local commissioners to opt out of the tax increases, without much opposition or discourse. And you know that local officials will quickly open a pipeline of propaganda about the inequitable hardships of the legislation.

They will plead with the public to understand how difficult it will be to cut back on spending, and how it will inevitably impact vital services such as police, fire, and emergency protection.

There is plenty of fat to cut from our budgets. Local businesses and the real-estate industry and residents are starving for a tax cut. Why not allow us to have a little caviar -- in the way of a tax cut -- with our champagne.

Florida Lawmakers' Big Bet   /May 2011

When Congress reduced taxes on stock dividends and capital gains several years ago, it was targeted at invigorating the U.S. markets.

The recent moves by Florida legislators to lower property taxes and insurance costs have a similar intent. It is hopeful that real-estate activity will be revived to the flourishing levels of past years.

Florida has an extraordinary economy. Its pillar is the clean, predictable industry of tourism. Attractions such as warm weather, beaches, and Disney World ensure that tourists continue to come.

The state economy has also been boosted by a steady influx of new residents, who buy goods and services -- as well as homes, second homes, and investment properties. This has proven to be lucrative commerce for the state.

However, the perfect storm of high property values, skyrocketing taxes, and limited and costly insurance has threatened the Florida real-estate market. State legislators see this as plain as our blue skies and sunshine.

The tax-cut package passed this month is intended to jolt the system with reform. The tax cuts are immediate and mandated to local cities, counties and other taxing boards.

Property taxes have continually risen in the state, often faster than increases in population. This has been particularly true here in Nassau County. Rampant spending on the county level has been the norm here.

Tax relief would be a breath of fresh air for everyone. And the public appears willing to speak out passionately about the tax situation.

Here are excerpts from readers' e-mails that followed a column last week about the tax cuts -- and how local officials are able to vote their way out of many of the measures (with super-majority votes):

One reader said in regard to the recent column, "Thank you for being a sane voice in this tax fiasco."

Another reader commented about the likelihood that local officials will initiate a propaganda campaign about the hardships of the tax cuts: "Just this day, I told my wife to be prepared for 'wailing and gnashing of teeth.'"

Yet another reader regurgitated some statistics used by a new commissioner in his election campaign. A graph in the election flier showed that the county's population increased 23 percent between 1997 and 2004 -- while tax revenues here went up by 121 percent.

But worse yet, county spending grew by 146 percent, meaning commissioners spent more than they brought in, even with the inflated level of revenues. The graph carried a headline: "We've got to stop SPENDING MORE than we collect." This is so true.

While tax reductions will inevitably cause some reduced services for residents, they are imperative for the health of the state's economy. High costs can choke off any business activity. The ancillary costs most near to real estate are taxes and insurance.

By reducing these costs, a positive spin will be placed on real estate in Florida. It will help existing residents, as well as new ones. Just as it did for the stock markets several years ago -- with the changes on dividends and gains.

A Workshop That Works   /September 2007

If you feel that Highway A1A in Yulee is scenic and idyllic and well-planned, then the date of October 3 should mean nothing to you.

Heck, take the evening and frolic across acres of asphalt-covered parking lots. Stop to rest by a retention pond or under one of the skinny, man-placed trees bordering the highway. And don't worry about lights if it gets dark. There are enough neon bulbs in some areas to light up a block of Las Vegas.

If, however, you feel the vital corridor between Amelia Island and Callahan is a hodgepodge of this and that -- and looks more like Blanding Boulevard every day -- you should attend an important meeting.

County officials will be reviewing rules for future development, particularly along A1A, in a workshop at 6 p.m., October 3 at the commission chambers (behind the Merita bread store). The workshop will have wide ramifications.

Officials will discuss environmental topics such as: requiring vegetative buffers along A1A; placement of retention ponds; buffers between development and wetlands; tree-protection laws (that have teeth); landscape provisions for future "big box" retailers; and handling of scenic, canopied roads.

For some time now, county officials have been shaping future land-development codes and the impact on natural resources. They want a unified book of codes that is usable and useful and a one-stop resource.

The workshop will provide a forum for input. Many times, officials use the turnout at such workshops as a barometer of whether issues are important or relevant to the public. The wording of many of these new codes will be important, as much so as putting a "will" versus a "will not" in the text. One word can present an obstacle, or a platform, for which someone can contest an issue.

So come out and be heard – and shape the future of A1A and Nassau County.

Part Two: Finance

No Crystal Ball   /March 2004

If you could equip yourself with one tool as an investor, the choice may be obvious. A crystal ball. You know, a tiny sphere of clairvoyance to guide you through the maze of investments available these days.

Just think. You could've navigated through the stock market crash of October 1987, the technology stock bubble of the late 1990s and the more recent bear market that forced some people out of retirement.

Of course, the real world calls. Crystal balls are purely fictional. And nobody can forecast with any certainty which asset class will outperform in a given time period.

Therefore, an investor is normally best served to spread out his investments between various assets – a strategy known as diversification. Instead of putting all your eggs in one carton, so to speak.

Over the last 25 years, U.S. stocks generally outperformed most other asset groups. However, this past year was the first time this had occurred since 1999. In between, a wrenching bear market sent many U.S. stocks tumbling and many other asset groups soaring – such as stocks in emerging markets.

After the general successes of U.S. stocks for the most of the 1990s, this would have been difficult to foresee. There are other surprises when you reflect on the general performance of the following groups over the last 25 years: U.S. large company stocks, U.S. small company stocks, international stocks, emerging market stocks, U.S. corporate bonds, non-U.S. bonds, and cash.

Who would have predicted this (returns are based upon indexes of these respective groups):

- Large company stocks in the U.S. led all other asset groups in performance four times during that period. But this was in four consecutive years – from 1995 to 1998 during the technology craze. No other time did this group provide the best returns.
- Corporate bonds in the U.S. provided the highest returns four times; in 1982, 1984, 2001 and 2002.

- Small company stocks in the U.S. led the way four times also. These years were in 1979, 1980, 1983 and 1992.
- Foreign stocks (those outside the U.S.) outperformed the other groups three times, 1985, 1986 and 1994.
- Stocks in emerging markets (those less developed) have turned in top performances a surprising number of times. It must be noted, however, that these markets tend to be more volatile and can experience significant declines in value. These also have not been tracked as long as other markets. The emerging markets led in 1988, 1989, 1991, 1993, 1999 and 2003.
- Non-U.S. bonds provided the best returns in three years (1987, 1990 and 2002). Each of these years witnessed a significant pullback in U.S. stocks.
- Cash, as measured by U.S. treasury bonds, outperformed only once during the last 25 years. This was in 1981, when interest rates soared and U.S. equity markets struggled through a trying time.

So there it is, in black and white. You would have needed a crystal ball to know how the last 25 years would unfold.

Greenspan's Chilling Words   /February 1996

The words rang out like a gunshot on a still, snow-covered night.

Alan Greenspan's innuendo that the U.S. stock market may be at an excessive valuation due to "irrational exuberance" shot down the recent rally. For a day or so, anyhow.

But should Wall Street be worried – like the Federal Reserve chairman seems to be suggesting?

A review of the low-inflation, high-earnings environment in the U.S. reveals the current valuations are normal, based against history. According to statistics from a prominent investment house, stocks often carry higher valuations in low-inflation periods.

Therefore, based upon historical contexts, the current valuation in the market is normal – in the type of environment that exists today.

As inflation pushes up interest rates, investors are often likely to slide over into the fixed-income markets and capitalize on the higher yields – than to bid up stocks. This behavior typically accompanies a bear market.

In addition, there are a few other factors that "bear" watching in today's market.

The first and foremost is inflation, and interest rates. In the past year, when rates have dropped below 7 percent on the long bond (the 30-year treasury), the stock market has roared. The long bond is now around a 6.60 percent yield. A sharp spike in rates of a point or more – caused by Greenspan or anything else – may spur a sell-off in stocks.

Also, with the U.S. economy anticipated to slow in the next two years, it would stand to reason that corporate profits would also decline. A succession of low earnings numbers – and subsequent forecasts – in bigger, blue-chip stocks could also trouble the market.

Whatever the intent, Greenspan's words seemed to chill the markets like a polar vortex last week – in the U.S. and abroad.

Wild Day on Wall Street   /May 2010

Computers have reshaped and reconstructed our lives –
with the precision of a surgeon's scalpel and with the speed of light.

Technological advancements have spurred on space travel,
medical discoveries and military breakthroughs. However, in what
seemed like a nanosecond, a computer-driven trading system nearly
crashed the U.S. stock market.

A near 1,000-point drop last Thursday on the Dow Jones
Industrial Average left spectators and participants aghast. "The
machines just took over," said one market trader. "There's not a lot
of human interaction."

Between 2:30 p.m. and 2:46 p.m., the Dow Jones index
plummeted more than 700 points in a bolt of lightning. Millions
and millions of shares of stock schizophrenically traded hands.
With today's modern, sophisticated trading systems, shares can
trade at blurring, numbing speeds.

In monetary terms, $800 billion in equity was lost in the
downturn – and $600 billion was restored in the rally. This was a
roller coaster that left the tracks and suddenly emerged intact.

It will be remembered as one of the wildest days in Wall
Street history. But it was a particularly tense 38-minute block of
time that few will forget.

When Greenspan Talks /March 1997

When Alan Greenspan talks, people listen. Stock and bond markets stir. And investors scramble to decipher the meaning of his words.

The past two weeks are a perfect example.

In the first segment of his twice-annual Humphrey Hawkins testimony, the Federal Reserve chairman plainly said the U.S. stock market is too high. He spoke much more directly to that point than he did in December when he made an off-handed comment during a speech about the potential of "irrational exuberance" among U.S. investors.

Greenspan rocked the markets for four days. Based on the hawkish tone, many market strategists figured a hike in interest rates would be almost imminent and around the corner.

But then, in a dramatic disclaimer, Greenspan rephrased what he had said while speaking to a business group last week. He said he meant the stock market is too high only if company earnings cannot support these levels.

And the stock and bond markets rebounded the latter part of last week. There are a few different ways to view this reversal of tone.

First, there are some who say the media has continually misinterpreted and sensationalized and exaggerated Greenspan's comments. Some say Greenspan was merely speaking for the Federal Reserve as a group, when he made his initial comments about the stock market's heights.

And last week's comments were more his feelings – that the market and the economy are doing quite well on their own as long as earnings stay high and inflation remains low.

Thirdly, there are those who feel Greenspan is doing nothing but jawboning the stock market back to a more-sustainable level. His words and comments can rile the markets.

Regardless, market watchers will continue to listen. And the stir is probably only beginning.

Sizzling Mutual Funds   /November 1995

Picking a mutual fund to invest in from all of those available is like deciding what to put on your plate at a "Taste of Amelia" dining event.

The annual taste-testing extravaganza offers food from 30 or so eateries and chefs from around Amelia Island. Choosing what to eat is the most difficult part of the evening.

It can be like that with mutual funds. There are many tempting kinds, with varying investments strategies, managers and structures. And you are bombarded with advertisements of a "hot fund" that has done remarkably during a selected period.

Then there is the task of monitoring the funds you choose, while blending them with other complementary funds for diversification. If you are fortunate enough to pick a top fund over a given period, then doing it again is often difficult. An analysis from the book, "A Random Walk Down Wall Street" by author Burton Malkiel, confirmed this.

Of the top-performing equity-based mutual funds in the 1970s, how many repeated in the top spots in the 1980s? If you think the number of repeat performers is high, you guessed as wrongly as the Iraqi military leaders. Only 17 percent of the top-performing funds from 1970-1979 maintained the highest rankings in the period from 1980-1989.

Now, not all of the mutual funds currently standing were around during that period. Many funds have been started during crazes in the markets over the last 10 years. How many new technology funds were created during the peak of the bull market of 1990s, for instance? (The answer: too many.)

Also, not all funds invest in equities, or stocks. There are mutual funds that invest in bonds – corporate, government, convertible, or high yield – for instance. Other funds focus on international stocks or bonds, while some currently popular funds specialize in shorting the market or buying into neutrally performing assets such as gold or currencies or real estate.

In the study in his book, Malkiel looked at the 177 equity funds (those that invest solely in stocks) in existence from the 1970s, and then watched how they did in the 1980s.

Of the 17 funds in the top 10 percent in the 1970s, only three repeated in that top tier in the '80s. Hence, he drew his conclusion that it is difficult for a fund to continue a torrid pace in terms of performance for a prolonged period of time.

Other studies have graded the performance of a portfolio that buys into the hottest fund of each year, and holds it for a year. The results, as you might guess, are often not that impressive.

One reason is that the hottest funds often fall in a hot sector. And a specific sector will not usually remain as the top-performing investment for an extended period.

So, in conclusion, whet your palate with information about the multitude of investment options out there. Choose cautiously, wisely.

And control your appetite.

Stock Market Correction? /April 1997

Can the U.S. economy be in such good shape that it becomes bad at some point?

That's a question many investors are asking, in the wake of the recent 500-point sell-off in the stock market (as measured in the Dow Jones Industrial Average), triggered at least in part by the Federal Reserve's decision to raise short-term interest rates.

The move by the Fed and powerful Chairman Alan Greenspan was posed as a preemptive strike against inflation. Too much of a good thing (a strong economy) can lead to more spending, higher prices – and alas, inflation.

So the answer is that too much of a good thing in the economy can become bad.

The Fed can raise interest rates to make money more expensive. These higher rates are passed along to the public through U.S. banks. This can dramatically affect home building, business expansions, lending, etc.

In this way, higher rates could begin to cool the economy – like tapping the brakes in a car. And elevated rates can impact the profitability of U.S. companies, since it becomes more expensive to access capital or refinance debt.

Also with higher rates available on fixed-income investments such as CDs, bonds, and preferred stocks, there is additional competition for money.

The timing of the Fed's move is interesting. Most of the inflationary pressures seen in the economy, such as in wages and the work force – are in their early stages. However, that is the time for the Fed to act, to stifle these trends before they begin accelerating (like they did in the early 1980s).

So, through all the turmoil in the stock market of late, there may be a silver lining. Remember back to 1994. It was a miserable year for both the stock and bond markets, caused mostly by successive rates hikes by the Fed. Most investors came through 1994 with some scars and bruises, but at least with minimal gains in their portfolios.

The payoff has been 1995 and 1996, two outstanding years in the markets.

It's difficult to predict that this is a replay of 1994, since there are some dramatic differences. One of the biggest is that interest rates were lower at the outset of the rate hikes in 1994, meaning they had to be raised six or seven times to reach a level that cooled the economy.

Long-term rates were already at 6.50 percent when the Fed decided to act this year. This could mean that rates will not need to be raised as many times.

All in all, the Dow's decline to the 6500 levels still leaves it 500 points above its November level, when it broke 6000 for the first time. That means there still has been about a 10 percent advance in the markets over the last five months.

That is good, by historical standards. And too much good, even in the case of rising stock prices, can eventually turn bad – in the form of a correction.

Many experts feel we could be getting close.

An Interest Rate Spike   /July 1997

The short but sudden spike in interest rates this past week sent shivers through the spines of investors – as a memory resurfaced of something 10 years ago.

It was like the worst of bad dreams.

The move in interest rates sent the U.S. stock and bond markets reeling for a day or so. However, the circumstances today appear to have little in common with that memorable time – the stock market crash of October 1987

In fact, interest rates in the fall of 1987 went from 8 to 10 percent in about three months, while stocks continued to rally. So the two markets – bonds and stocks – sort of decoupled.

Beginning in August 1987, interest rates began creeping up from the 8 percent area – and reached the double-digit level in a sudden burst.

Today, interest rates are hovering around 6.50 percent. While the move last week – of about a quarter-point – sent interest rates (as measured by the 30-year treasury) slightly higher, it hardly measures in magnitude with what happened in 1987.

In addition, the earnings of U.S. companies across the board have been stellar in recent months. This in turn has driven stock valuations to high levels.

And while interest rates turned the other way last week, they had been falling with consistency. This has been part of a strong rally in the bond market.

If you graphed the stock market's performance for the three years leading up to 1987, and compared it to the three-year period from 1994 to today, the results are astonishingly similar. Both were strong bull markets.

So with valuations high, interest rates require watching. Especially as we move within 100 days of the 10-year anniversary of the worst one-day decline in history.

The day the stock market dropped 500 points – or 22 percent.

The facts beneath the surface appear different this time, however. And as long as earnings are better and interest rates are lower, what has happened in the last few years will hopefully continue to happen.

And not relive October 1987.

One Terrific Party /August 1996

It was a terrific party.

From January 1995 to this past May, the U.S. stock market had been on a rip-roaring run, with investor enthusiasm reaching euphoric levels. This has suddenly changed, with stock prices falling from the May peaks to the July troughs.

Recent losses have turned greed to fear. In fact, it seems almost schizophrenic how quickly conversations changed from how high the latest IPO (initial public offering) could climb to whether or not this selloff was the "big one." Thus, life goes on in the stock market.

Now the big question is whether the quick, but hard-hitting, correction is over. And whether investors should climb out of the protective foxholes they have dug for themselves.

In hindsight, it is now easy to see that the classic signs of investor greed were present in May; this typically signals the market has neared a top. Tell-tale signs were a red-hot IPO market; near-record valuations of stocks; money leaving cash and other stable fixed-income investments to chase soaring stocks; distant relatives crowing about their investment prowess.

Now, the mood surrounding stocks has dimmed to a more subdued level. And sometimes this can portend a rally.

The IPO market has fizzled. This is considered to be a barometer of investor sentiment. In fact, similar readings of the IPO market over the past three months are synonymous with the readings posted near the bottom of the 1992 and 1994 corrections.

Another relevant indicator – investors' enthusiasm for technology stocks – also signals caution. Investors have had as much love for technology stocks as the Hatfields had for the McCoys.

And the valuations of growth stocks (like technology) have declined substantially. Growth stocks usually belong to companies in the earlier stages of development, which often carry high valuations.

Therefore, the stocks of many small-cap and mid-cap companies have been reduced to reasonable levels and valuations. (You could say they have been discounted.)

Lastly, managers of many growth-stock mutual funds continue to keep high levels of cash in their portfolios. Usually, these cautious levels are associated with the conclusion of a correction.

All this having been said, the question is still whether the correction is done. Only time will tell – when this party is over.

An Acronym with Meaning /January 1996

If your retirement nest egg consists of a savings bond you keep inside a dusty book, a bank account paying 2 percent, and a collection of Beatles albums, you need to read further.

You also should read further if you are doing it right, paying part of your income each month into a company retirement plan, and embellishing that with a sizable stock and bond portfolio. Because there is one vehicle that nicely complements both of these situations.

It is an IRA, or Individual Retirement Account.

Planning for retirement is a lifelong, and complex, process. Your IRA is a foundation upon which you can build the rest of the plan. There are a few things that set an IRA apart.

First, your money grows tax-deferred. That means you don't pay taxes on your interest and gains until you withdraw the money. This allows for a unique compounding effect, since your interest and gains are not taxed each year (if left inside the IRA).

Another popular feature of an IRA was changed a number of years ago. Participants in company retirement plan may not be able to deduct IRA contributions from their taxes. But that does not mean you should no longer contribute each year.

For one thing, Congress is toying around with making changes to IRAs. This could mean allowing more to be contributed per year, for instance.

And good luck if you are counting on Social Security benefits to pay for your retirement. The Social Security Administration estimates those benefits will replace only one-third of your pre-retirement income.

Of even more concern, there have been whispers by Congress of the existing Social Security system being underfunded by around 2020.

Also consider contributing to your IRA earlier each year (rather than waiting until April 15), so that your money has longer to grow tax-deferred. When you play this out over 20 or 30 years, the additional interest and gains could be substantial.

By no means will an IRA necessarily finance your entire retirement. But it is a critical piece of the pie – that can add flavor to your retirement.

Investors Lag in Returns /February 1998

It's an intriguing concept: investment returns are different from investor returns.

The statement is from Nick Murray, a celebrated speaker on financial topics. The proof is from a study by the Morningstar rating service, which uses a popular star system to rank mutual funds.

The startling report by Morningstar showed the average investment returns of 219 growth-oriented mutual funds (those investing in stocks) was 12.5 percent annually during the five-year period between May 31, 1989, and May 31, 1994. That means these funds turned in an impressive performance.

However, investors' returns in the same 219 funds was -2.5 percent (as in a minus, or negative, return) in the same period. That means the typical investor in these funds lost money by getting in – and especially out – at the wrong times.

How could this happen, you ask, peeking up from the pages of Money magazine with those graphic ads proclaiming blockbuster mutual-fund returns? Read on.

While mutual funds are a popular investment vehicle, the returns are based upon when you get in – and how long you stay in. This is the problem.

Too many investors use mutual funds as trading vehicles, jumping in and out, trying to time the market's ups and downs with the futility of a one-armed wallpaper hanger. So just because a mutual fund's returns were 12.5 percent per year doesn't mean you got that return. Especially if you were hastily jumping in and out on every dip in the stock market.

The Morningstar report reflects this. The study looked at flows of money into and out of the 219 funds. Obviously, more money was going in after the funds' performances peaked (as appears to be happening now), and money flowed out after the funds' values had dropped.

The opposite is the key to good investing. As in the trite buy-low, sell-high philosophy.

However, mutual funds are not trading vehicles. They are long-term investments that can provide stellar returns – if you get in and stay in, through good markets as well as bad.

In this way, your returns can possibly keep up with – rather than lag – the markets.

Markets Move with Developments /May 1998

The noise is deafening. Stifling. And at times, frightening.

Trade wars with Japan. U.S. warships speeding toward the Persian Gulf. The Asian economic flu. And through it all, investors try to keep their eyes focused on the horizon of their financial goals.

All three have been global news items recently, moving the markets with each development. But in the big picture of the U.S. markets, they have once again proven to be overblown and over-exaggerated.

The supposed "trade wars" were resolved in a day or two. And the disagreement involved only four Japanese companies – not all of Japan. The possibility of the U.S. sanctions against these companies developing into a trade war seemed to be a stretch. And it was.

The tensions in the volatile and oil-rich Persian Gulf are legitimate. And likely to continue. The concern here is the oil – and oh yes, the potential ramifications of U.S. military forces being used to settle a no-fly-zone violation. Fears of another Arab oil embargo reverberated.

But again, nothing.

Now the Asian flu epidemic hit hard and fast. It rocked the stock market, dropping it 800 points over three days. Fears ran wild over potential effects on the U.S. markets and earnings of companies here. And again, things settled down.

So let's get down to what matters most within the stock market. Earnings. Expectations. And inflation/interest rates.

Earnings drive stock prices. The more profitable a company, the better Wall Street normally likes it. However, the earnings have to be predictable and measure up to what Wall Street analysts are expecting.

While earnings are concrete and reported every quarter, expectations are a little bit more esoteric. This entails what a company is expected to earn and do in the future, based upon new products, new technology, etc.

High expectations can carry stocks to exaggerated valuations, regardless of the earnings in many cases. However, the earnings have to come through in due time, or else the bubble of expectations will burst – and the stock price will fall.

And lastly, but every bit as importantly, interest rates. These are driven by the buying and selling in the bond market – and by inflationary pressures.

Inflation is the increase or perceived increase in prices and the costs of living. High inflation is typically bad. It normally accompanies or causes higher interest rates and prices. Most declining stock markets in the U.S. have been accompanied by a spike-up in interest rates.

So these conditions deserve watching. While you do less listening to the noise.

Investors Can't Hide /December 1997

They used to think the world was flat. That is, until a wily Christopher Columbus proved otherwise.

People also used to believe that they were protected from external influences from around the globe if they invested in big, so-called safe companies inside the U.S. stock market. That has also changed.

Global developments impact the U.S. financial markets like never before. And as Columbus probably told his naysayers, "You haven't seen anything yet."

The latest incident has been imported from Asia. Not only did the U.S. stock market feel a slap of global reality and sell off nearly 15 percent (from its previous high) in October due to the imported Asian difficulties, but still today you hear companies lament about weaknesses in their earnings due to Asia's slowdown and uncertainties.

A major company that manufactures equipment for semiconductor chips has announced a foreseeable slowdown in earnings due to the effects of Asia. They are just the latest. Different types of companies from very different sectors have done the same.

And investors might as well get used to it, and brace themselves and their portfolios for more from Asia over the next three to six months. Companies with Asian exposure will remain vulnerable to bad news from that region – although this has been priced in to some stocks.

There is much talk about Asian companies trying to export themselves out of the financial mess, meaning they would reduce prices on their products – such as cars, computers and electronics – and this would drive down prices here. This in turn could affect the earnings of U.S. companies and the overall economy here.

Again, the global economy rears its complex head. Other external influences are also present, most notably the political tensions in Iraq. The underlying implication here is on oil – and oil prices.

A few years ago, the Mexican peso devalued. And this contributed to a poor stock market in the U.S. in 1994.

The Arab oil embargo. The Gulf War. These external forces each impacted the U.S. stock market.

So the moral here is that an investor must keep one eye on the U.S. economy and one eye outside our borders. The global economy is here and growing.

Someday, with behemoths such as McDonald's and Coke relying so heavily on their operations around the world for future growth, the global economy could almost become the prevailing theme. Factors relating to the U.S. economy would be part of the overall picture.

Already, as we sleep, the performances of stock markets in Asia and Europe impact the U.S. market. So, in your waking hours, watch and listen to these world developments.

It'll help you sleep that much better.

Financial Buffet for Buffett   /August 2008

The state of Florida has a great deal for you – if your last name is Buffett.

In a deal that appears fairly one-sided, Warren Buffett's company received $224 million to pledge to loan the state up to $4 billion if a hurricane causes catastrophic damage here this year. But it gets better.

Buffett would receive tax-free bonds backed by the state of Florida for the amount of the loan. And the bonds would pay a desirable 6.50 percent interest rate to Buffett's company, Berkshire Hathaway.

Now that's a deal only desperate politicians and a shrewd businessman could arrange.

Gov. Charlie Crist contends the state may not be able to absorb the financial damages from a major hurricane. Due to tight credit markets, the state might be unable to borrow such a large sum after a catastrophe, or pay a higher rate. Crist knows Buffett's guarantee is there if needed.

So he and other officials signed the agreement with Buffett. Attorney General Bill McCollum opposed the deal, contending the terms were overly favorable for Buffett's side.

"It is a $224 million opportunity for Berkshire Hathaway to make money on us," McCollum says. "I just don't think it's a good deal for the state."

While forecasters are calling for a busy hurricane season, the odds are low that a disastrous storm will strike Florida. McCollum says there is only a 3 to 4 percent chance the state would need the funds from Buffett. McCollum feels the federal government would provide low-interest loans if a severe storm hits anyhow.

On the contrary, Crist says the guarantee from Buffett will allow him to sleep better at night. With a tropical storm bearing down on Florida right now, maybe Crist's intuitions are sound.

However, the terms are overly favorable to Buffett. Berkshire Hathaway receives the $224 million simply for the pledge to loan the funds – which would be at a pristine rate. "Berkshire Hathaway will wind up pocketing the money," McCollum says.

The bonds are backed by the state, which gives them a stellar credit rating against default. The bonds would mature over 30 years; their interest would be paid from assessments on insurance policies.

Crist's concern lies with the state's hurricane insurance fund. The fund, with only $8 billion in cash right now, provides backstop coverage for insurance companies beset with sizable losses after a hurricane.

If storm-related losses exceed $25 billion, the state could borrow funds from Buffett. The $224 million paid to Buffett was taken from the hurricane insurance fund's reserves.

As a billionaire investor with hordes of cash, Buffett can dictate favorable terms on deals. He has been putting other funds to work in similar capacities within an uncertain financial environment.

Crist says he would prefer to spend the millions of dollars on education or teachers, but he feels preparing for disaster is most important. The state struggled in 2005 to issue similar tax-free bonds after the rash of storms.

At least now Crist can sleep. While Buffett dreams up another sweet deal.

Japan Has Taste for Treasuries /March 1997

With Tokyo investors losing their taste for Japanese stocks as if they were soured sushi, concerns have loomed about the impact on the U.S. financial markets.

But as the Nikkei Average in Tokyo sagged to the 17,000 level last week, the U.S. stock market continued to rally – and set record highs. So there seems to be little resemblance or correlation between the two major stock markets right now.

The biggest difference between the U.S. and Japan is economic health. The U.S. has it; in comparison, Japan's economy is in a financial coma.

In fact, Japan is plagued by a banking crisis that makes the prior U.S. savings and loan debacle seem trivial. And the once-mighty Japanese economy is as slow-moving as an old Datsun.

Meanwhile, the U.S. economy continues to grow in a healthy, low-inflationary environment. And American businesses, strengthened by years of cost cutting and restructuring, are growing and expanding – and in many cases, dominating the world in their fields.

With interest rates as low as they are in Japan, it makes sense that the Japanese are buying higher-yielding U.S. treasuries, helping our bond market. Likewise, money continues to flow from overseas into the soaring U.S. stock market. It would also stand to reason that money might be flowing from Japanese to U.S. stocks.

However, the substantial decline in the Nikkei in recent years is a bit disconcerting. The thought of a near 50-percent decline occurring here, as it has in Japan, can provide a cold slap of reality for the investor who fears U.S. stocks have gone too far, too fast.

But Japan's stock-market rally reached unrealistic heights on rampant speculation. At the top of the Nikkei's surge, investors were leveraging even their real estate holdings to get more money to buy stocks.

Despite an inference to euphoria in the U.S. stock market made by Federal Reserve Chairman Alan Greenspan, hardly has the enthusiasm here reached the levels of Japan's heyday.

One common theme does exist between the two stock markets, however. As technical analyst Alan Shaw has demonstrated, the U.S. bull market of the last 15 years greatly resembles on a chart the Nikkei's push beyond 30,000 – with one major difference.

If charts of the two bull markets are laid side by side, the similarities are striking, except for the U.S. surge encompassing about half of the Nikkei's.

If true, that could set the tone for a continued rise in the U.S. stock market (corrections are normal occurrences within a bull market). And if this comparison by Shaw plays out, the same type of crisis occurring in Japan could occur here in the U.S., at some point down the road.

That provides some food for thought. Meanwhile, pass the sushi. Let's eat and be merry. The U.S. bull market still has a long way to go – if Japan's path is one we follow.

But let's certainly change the conclusion.

What Experts Might Say /February 1998

The Asian economic contagion. Three consecutive years in which the U.S. stock market has produced returns of more than 20 percent. A projected slowdown in earnings of American companies.

These are the major reasons for many experts offering subdued forecasts for the U.S. stock market in 1998.

With earnings of U.S. companies already projected to decline against a backdrop of slower economic growth, the Asian meltdown is not timely. Asian countries will most likely try to export themselves out of their financial messes. This means reducing prices to be competitive.

In turn, prices in many areas are almost certain to come under pressure from the additional competition.

There could be a saving grace, however. The Asian turmoil has probably forced the Federal Reserve to sit on the sidelines. Many believe the Fed would have raised interest rates toward the end of last year had the Asian crisis not persisted. And higher interest rates can negatively impact companies.

In addition, some market watchers are saying the Fed may even consider lowering interest rates if the Asian flu proves worse than feared. This type of move would help stimulate our now-booming economy – should it sag from the Asian situation splashing cold water on it.

Never before has the U.S. stock market produced three straight years of 20 percent returns (as measured by most indexes). If history has its way, this year could be sub-par.

The U.S. economy, heading into its eighth year of expansion, must eventually take a breather. Nothing in the economic world goes straight up. An expansion of six or seven years is unusual; anything more is unlikely in a historical context.

If the U.S. economy slows, then corporate profits are likely to also decline. The projected slowdown in corporate earnings is based upon this logic. Lower earnings eventually should be reflected in lower stock prices.

Investors should be uplifted by the interest-rate picture, however. Interest rates, based upon the long bond or benchmark

30-year treasury, have fallen dramatically over the last six months – to about 5.75 percent. This has been favorable for stocks.

Lower interest rates can make it cheaper for companies to operate as well as expand. And nearly all bear, or declining, markets in U.S. stocks have been accompanied or caused by a spike-up in interest rates.

As for now, rates appear to be heading lower.

While this hardly paints a rosy picture, remember one other thing. The U.S. economy is stream-rolling right now. Interest rates are low. Earnings of American companies are still high within a bull market. These are facts.

Everything else mentioned here is based upon projections or popular opinions from so-called experts. And these may – or may not – play out. Remember that these are only opinions.

When Baby Boom Booms /September 1998

Harry Dent sees an economic boom ahead – of sonic proportions.

Dent, a widely followed economist, forecasts the U.S. stock market will ride the wave of Baby Boomers turning 50. And this wave is tidal in nature.

As people turn 50, they enter their peak spending years, according to Dent. And with the Baby Boom generation – the size and scope of which the U.S. has never before seen – now entering its 50s, the spending on cars and houses and vacations is peaking.

Dent predicts the spending wave will crest in the year 2008 and decline gradually through about 2015. But the massive spending on products made by American companies should help fuel their earnings for years to come.

Dent describes in "The Great Boom Ahead" that this monstrous generation could push the U.S. stock market to levels never before seen. It is the same type of demographic stimulus that pushed the Japanese stock market to the 36,000 level through the 1980s (the Japanese's "Baby Boom" generation peaked during that time).

And it is not simply that Baby Boomers are earning more and spending more. They are also buying stocks and pumping millions into their company retirement plans – which, yes, invest often in stocks. Just as Baby Boomers enjoy luxury items, they also seem to like the stock market.

In addition to these staggering numbers, a massive transfer of wealth will be taking place the next 15 years. This entails an estimated $10.4 trillion (according to a Cornell University study) passing from an older generation of savers to the Baby Boomers.

And Boomers are inclined to buy stocks – and not so much CDs and treasuries and savings bonds as their parents invested in with ironclad discipline.

Dent contends all this adds up to a projected move in the U.S. stock market that could rival Japan's of the 1980s. Dent has an illustration showing the aging of Baby Boomers and the movement of the stock market thus far. The common movements between the two are uncanny.

Dent says this is not by coincidence. And it will not subside anytime soon, based upon his research.

The bullish view has played out like a script since the early 1990s, when the first Boomers turned 50. And the market (based upon the Dow Jones Industrial Average) has gone through 4000, and 5000, and 6000 and 7000 – and now potentially 8000.

There is an eventual downside to this rosy, ever-promising picture for the stock market. That begins sometime after 2008 when the Baby Boomers begin to age into their later years and fade from the economic view. And a mammoth recession begins, Dent says.

But the tidal rise of the stock market between now and then should dwarf the recession Dent foresees culminating years later. In fact, you could say the recession will put little more than a dent in this booming market he projects.

Investors Watch Fed /April 1998

The question is whispered at dinner parties, bellowed in barber shops and broadcast through the media.

The $64 million question is whether the Federal Reserve Board will raise interest rates in its upcoming meeting; regardless of what month the meeting is, it is still a hotly debated issue.

Meanwhile, as traders and investors scurry to position themselves as the answer to the question flip-flops from side the side, the stock and bond markets swing. And sag. And skyrocket.

Not to get into an economic dissertation here, but the Fed's actions are closely watched and anticipated for a lot of reasons. First of all, the Fed's opinion on the markets matters. The 12-member board, directed by Chairman Alan Greenspan, is knowledgeable and in some ways a leading indicator of what lies ahead for the economy.

Interest rates are followed as closely as Saddam Hussein because they directly influence the bond market, which affects the stock market. And while rate hikes by the Fed will often douse the fire of rip-roaring markets, rate cuts by the board usually serve as fuel to a smoldering economy. So the Fed's action is critical.

It is often a mystery to people why interest rates matter so much. For one thing, most declines – and bear stock markets – in the last 30 years have been accompanied or preceded by a spike in interest rates. Take October 1987, for instance. The crash was preceded by a move in interest rates from 8 to 10 percent over a couple months.

When rates go higher, the conventional wisdom is that money is presumably tighter and that business operations (financing existing debt, borrowing new money, etc.) become more expensive, thus potentially hurting profits of companies.

Also, a bond market with higher yields presents competition to stocks. And some investors will flee stocks for the perceived sanctity of 10 percent bonds, for instance, in the case of 1987.

In addition, higher interest rates can give way to rampant inflation, which is bad for everything and everybody. Many people who fondly remember getting a 14-percent return on certificates of deposit in the early 1980s forget one important issue – inflation was running 12 percent. So your true gain, in terms of increased spending power, was 2 percent. (Oh yes, and then there are things called taxes.)

When the Fed raises or cuts interest rates (actually, they control the federal funds and discount rates – but these usually move rates overall), they often follow with another, successive move. So the markets also anticipate this, in the wake of the prior move.

The Fed raises rates for the basic reason that it sees an economy growing too fast – and potentially fueling inflation. Or, it perceives the economy struggling, and might reduce rates to free up money in the banking system (encouraging lending to consumers and businesses).

Thus, hopefully stoking an economic recovery. So there you have it. Some of the reasons why the Fed's actions are watched so closely.

Will they raise interest rates in their meeting later this month? With an election two months off and mixed signals thus far on the economy's growth and consumer sentiment (read between the lines here)?

Actually, your guess is as good as mine. But one thing can be assured – the question will continue to crop up. Anyhow, it makes for good television and conversation.

So pass the olives, please. And keep it short around the ears, with a little sideburn.

Saving America's Future /November 1997

The only thing depositing in your piggy bank is dust.

Your savings account is heading south faster than a snowbird in January. And those well-founded retirement plans, well, took a back seat to that new sports car.

No, you're probably not saving enough – or, at least not as much as you used to. One of the most disturbing trends that economists have tracked over the past 25 years has been the steady decline in the U.S. savings rate.

The savings rate of Americans has fallen from 7.7 percent of disposable income in the 1970s to 6.5 percent in the 1980s to only 4.5 percent in the 1990s. Moreover, this rate is the lowest among the major industrialized nations.

The reasons for this decline continue to baffle researchers, especially during a period when the U.S. government has offered many tax incentives for long-term savers. These include individual retirement accounts (IRAs) and 401K retirement plans for employees, Keogh plans for small business owners, and Simplified Employee Pension (SEP) plans for self-employed individuals.

Some of the culprits may be a reliance on government programs such as Social Security, Medicare and low-cost college loans. And credit is far easier to get these days, lulling people to accumulate debt at the expense of saving for a rainy day.

Even IRA contributions are declining. IRAs were first offered in 1974 as a means for citizens to save for retirement. These plans allow savers to shelter investment gains from taxes until they begin making withdrawals (normally after age 59 ½).

In 1990, contributions to IRAs totaled less than $10 billion – only one-fourth of what they were in 1986.

The decline in savings may mean that those golden retirement years could be tarnished. People may be forced to put off retirement, working longer than expected – and altering their futures.

Grandpa Goes Hi-Tech /November 1999

The grandfather of stock market indexes just got a new pair of high-tech running shoes.

In a move that validates the ongoing technology revolution, the Dow Jones Industrial Average added Microsoft and Intel to its revered 30-stock lineup and discarded some companies whose time had come – and noticeably gone.

Along with software-giant Microsoft and chip-producer Intel, the Dow also invited in telecommunications standout SBC and retailer Home Depot. However, Microsoft and Intel are the first two Dow components to trade on the new-wave NASDAQ – and that move attracted much publicity.

The Dow has changed dramatically over time. The index, which is used synonymously with "the market," tries to keep pace with changes in society and industry. Retailers such as the old Woolworth (removed from the index) and Wal-Mart recently changed places – a reflection of today's trends.

The Dow was given birth back in the late 1800s by journalist Charles Dow. Of the 12 original companies on the index, most were railroads, a reflection of the importance this mode of transportation had in building our nation.

Changes came as fast as a locomotive over the years. In fact, the only company still remaining from the original Dow list is General Electric. But even GE, a mammoth company today with 12 divisions that include jet engines and light bulbs and electric appliances, has obviously gone through a few changes (they didn't have jet engines in the late 1800s, did they?).

The Dow has a storied career. On Oct. 28 and 29, 1929, the Dow declined 12.8 percent and then 11.7 percent in what many identify as the beginning of the Great Depression.

But the index rolled on.

The Dow hobbled through the atomic bomb being dropped at Hiroshima in 1945, witnessed the first computer produced a year later at the University of Pennsylvania, and saw the Russians launch the world's first satellite in 1957. Each of these events triggered a new era – nuclear, computer and space.

In fact, the four companies removed from the Dow as of Nov. 1 – Sears, Union Carbide, Chevron and Goodyear Tire – each remind us from where our society has come. The old line retailer. A storied manufacturer. An oil giant. And a maker of tires.

And Microsoft and Intel show us where we are headed. A computer revolution, buoyed by the Internet craze, is upon us. And few companies have dominated their industries more than Microsoft and Intel.

In fact, Microsoft now has the largest market capitalization of any company (the number of shares outstanding multiplied by the price of its stock), larger than even … GE.

My, how times are changing.

Trip 'Round the World /December 1994

You turn off your Phillips television, phase out the picture on your NEC computer monitor and head out the door, jumping into your Volvo.

You've just taken a trip around the world, in the sense that these products are all made by foreign companies.

And if you use these products, it's likely that your neighbors, other residents of your town, and people around the U.S. and the world do also. Just as you invested your money in these products, you can also invest in the companies that manufacture them – through the stock markets of the world.

Today only 38 percent of the stocks available in the world are tied to U.S. companies. The other 62 percent come from companies overseas.

It stands to reason that a balanced investment portfolio will have some overseas exposure to capitalize on this. By putting money into foreign investments, whether they are individual stocks or bonds, or mutual funds with an international flavor, you can potentially reduce volatility.

That's because if the U.S. stock market drops, other markets around the world will not necessarily decline. This was illustrated in a study that showed that by diversifying into overseas markets in the last 10 years, you not only increased your returns – but also reduced fluctuations in your portfolio.

In addition, the world's bond markets are changing and have grown rapidly in the last 10 years. In 1983, the U.S. government bond market represented 58 percent of all the bonds in the world; by the end of 1993, the U.S. bond presence fell to 46 percent.

While global investing provides more opportunities, there are risks. These include currency fluctuations, differing standards for disclosing financial conditions of companies (making it difficult to research them), and low liquidity and a lack of oversight in some foreign markets.

All this being said, the simplest way to approach the foreign markets is often through international or foreign mutual funds.

Here, you essentially hire a money manager to buy and sell the securities for you.

Also, this can give you exposure to various foreign markets with one convenient investment. And hopefully help reduce the turbulence of your trip around the world.

Part Three: Economics

Economy Gets Sour Stomach   /August 2011

A proven recipe for souring the appetite of an upstart economy contains two key ingredients: A) raising taxes B) increasing regulations.

Currently, in the U.S., we have a little and a lot of each. A little in regard to higher income taxes (most of the increases have been through expanded fees and silent taxes). And a lot in terms of new regulations. A very lot.

With the national unemployment rate sticking to a 9 percent level, the most discussed and debated four-letter word in the English language has been "jobs." A much-publicized speech last week by President Obama focused on government-driven programs for putting Americans back to work.

A temporary work-start program could have a short-term impact. But longer term, the tested method to jumpstart the economy and to get businesses hiring again is to remove the barriers presented by a logjam of regulations.

Noted financial experts such as Mario Gabelli are drawing attention to this. In an interview, Gabelli asserted that it would be impossible to start a thriving financial business like his in today's environment. Too much red tape. Too much government intervention. Too much uncertainty.

The Sarbanes-Oxley Act of 2002 and the evolving Dodd-Frank Consumer Protection Act are providing bookends of resistance to new and existing businesses. In fact, the Dodd-Frank bill is still being finalized. It was passed several years ago, but the blanks in the framework are now being filled out with terms of uncertainty.

One of the fastest-growing banks in the U.S. -- with a substantial presence in North Florida -- is doing little right now. A top representative said the bank is "sitting on its hands" and waiting for several major regulations to be spawned off of the Dodd-Frank evolution. The bank is servicing existing loans, but offering few new ones.

Some regulation is necessary to prevent another financial meltdown like in 2008. But often, the pendulum swings too far in the other direction -- at a time when the economy is struggling to recover from a major recession like the one we just had.

There are other instances of increased regulation:

- The National Labor Board's attempt to block a non-unionized Boeing plant from being built in South Carolina.

- The federal Department of Justice's opposition to AT&T acquiring the T-Mobile USA cellular division from Deutsch Telecom. This is an instance of a U.S. company being prevented from acquiring a foreign competitor (while European companies seem unhindered in acquiring U.S. counterparts).

- The federal government lawsuit against 17 major banks for alleged misfeasance during the sub-prime mortgage debacle of three years ago.

And you wonder why large and small companies alike are not hiring? The U.S. Chamber of Commerce had a targeted response to the Obama jobs plan and other anti-business actions: Curb new regulations (such as those steeped in the new healthcare regulations).

Like him or not, Florida Gov. Rick Scott tabled any new regulations upon taking office, and ordered a review of existing ones -- especially those that pertain to the economy and much-needed job growth. Sounds like a recipe for growth, not disaster.

Maybe the pendulum is ready to swing to at least a more-neutral position.

Serving What People Want   /March 2007

Restaurants in downtown Fernandina Beach are hungry for new customers.

They are attempting to band together to promote themselves as a collective unit, unifying against the onslaught of popular chain restaurants opening here.

Just imagine: eat dinner at one restaurant, have dessert at another, and an after-dinner drink at the one down the street. All as part of a promotion to attract more diners to historic downtown.

Some businesses in Jacksonville, each in the home-repair and maintenance areas, are doing a similar thing. The call themselves the "Big Six," and they can repair or maintain your house from foundation to rooftop. One handles roof repairs, one does air-conditioning work, another specializes in tiling and flooring, and so on.

The six innovative businesses have one phone number, which gets routed according to your need. It's refreshing and inspiring that downtown restaurants are considering something along these lines.

Instead of competing, they will complement one another. The idea is to bring more diners to downtown, where the fine, locally owned restaurants are certainly enough to make your mouth water.

However, they cannot advertise as effectively or widely as chains such as Applebee's and even McDonald's. They also do not have the deep pockets of these national chains.

But with planning and cooperation, they can whet the palate of even the most-discerning diner. And get them coming back for seconds.

A Flood of Insurance Questions   /April 2007

Jekyll Island is located just north of Amelia Island, along the Southeastern Georgia coast.

More relevantly, it is situated in the middle of a political debate over new development and whether federally-backed flood insurance should protect it.

Jekyll Island is sparsely populated. Most of the land is government-owned and off-limits to development. Except for the Summer Waves water park and some bike trails and a few athletic fields, it offers few activities for residents and visitors. Its appeal is in its solitude.

This is apparently going to change. More than 600 new houses are planned for Jekyll Island in the near future. Though the number of houses is a drop in the ocean for busier locations such as Nassau County, it is significant because it draws attention to the debate over flood insurance, and whether new, at-risk construction should be extended the federal coverage.

For most people, even those living on the ocean, flood insurance is inexpensive. The federal government subsidizes the cost, and then picks up the tab when flood-related claims come pouring in after a disaster. There is also private flood insurance through companies such as Lloyd's of London, for instance, but it costs substantially more.

The debate centers on exactly that -- the federal government's expanding exposure to flood-related claims during times of catastrophic events. Look no farther than Hurricane Katrina's tragic imprint on the Gulf Coast.

The new Jekyll Island homes, along with several in Grayton Beach in the Florida Panhandle, were discussed during the recent session of Congress. Developments continually crop up along hazardous, flood-prone areas -- and federal officials are struggling with extending coverage to them.

Since its inception in 1968, the National Flood Insurance Program has grown in scale from 1.4 million policyholders to 5 million. But there is more. The total risk exposure (the value of insured property) is estimated at $900 billion.

Some federal officials feel this is too much risk -- for the government, and for taxpayers, who essentially fund many of the costs of the federal flood program, along with insurance companies, states, etc.

The debate began under President Reagan, when the Coastal Barrier Resources Act was passed. The act did not restrict where private landowners could build, but it mandated that the federal government would not subsidize such at-risk construction, whether through flood insurance, roads, etc.

A map delineating covered and non-covered areas was established. Since that time, the boundaries have been feverishly debated and often extended to include high-risk properties. The Jekyll Island houses fell under this debate.

Other barrier islands such as Amelia Island could also be affected if the federal government strictly enforces the boundaries of the barrier act, or simply limits flood insurance. In fact, many banks will not issue mortgages without flood insurance.

So the debate rages. While Jekyll Island and Grayton Beach are a distance away, the implications of the flood insurance tussle is hitting close to home.

The Development Craze   /February 2007

Cecil Field is getting a facelift -- from a military graveyard into a new, upscale shopping center the likes of St. Johns Town Center.

The old Gilman paper mill in St. Marys, Ga., will become a glitzy blend of residential and commercial landscapes. The tiny community of Briny Breezes, Florida, may have them all beat. The trailer-park town along the Atlantic Coast will reportedly be sold for $500 million and developed into condos, a luxury hotel, and marina.

However, there is a payoff for Briny Breezes residents, who must move from their seaside trailers as part of the deal. In return, each will reap about $1 million. The payoff is even more staggering, when you think that many bought their trailers for as little as $35,000.

The residents of Briny Breezes dramatically voted in favor of the all-or-none sale. The deal is still pending, however, and residents will not get paid until 2009. Still, the potential payout was irresistible for the owners of the 488 mobile homes on the idyllic 43-acre property reminiscent of old Florida.

The developer, Ocean Land Investments of Boca Raton, must still obtain zoning approval for the high-density project. There are concerns about evacuation routes and the likes for the crowded Atlantic corridor of Florida.

Briny Breezes began as a strawberry farm in the 1920s. It was acquired by a group of regular visitors, and converted into a town in 1963.

Cecil Field has a storied history among military circles. The base was closed in 1999. Since then, the city has tried to attract industry and commercial ventures to the property.

The proposed development from Tri-Star Commercial LLC would be bigger than the St. Johns Town Center. It would entail primarily retail outlets, providing a boost to a mostly downtrodden area.

Commercial developer LandMar is converting the old Gilman plant into a commercial/residential potpourri. Much of the equipment has been sold off, and a cleanup must ensue before development can begin.

LandMar's exploit is just another case of developers being eager to invest big bucks into valuable seaside or metropolitan areas. The same goes with Cecil Field's development and the enterprise of Briny Breezes.

This could be a lesson for local officials. The quaint downtown of Fernandina Beach -- and its deep water marina -- could certainly attract some type of major investment. (The $5 million the city borrowed to improve the marina is a pittance to what a major developer could bring to the waterfront.)

Just take Cecil Field, where the developers will hold a long-term lease on the land and pay the city a portion of their profits or a percentage of the appraised value of the project (once completed).

Instead of fighting developers, these are examples of using their deep pockets to benefit a community. No one could argue that the current state of Cecil Field is preferable to what the projected development will become.

No one could contend the dilapidated mill site in St. Marys is better than what LandMar will conceive. And though Briny Breezes is a storybook-type community, mobile homes pale to what the new developer will construct.

Business and government working together, hand in hand. For better, and sometimes for the worse.

But clearly for the better in the right instances.

Have You Heard of Jefferson? /April 2008

You might not know Jefferson County, Ala. by name. The county is anchored by the city of Birmingham, but it is now known for more than that.

It may become the next Orange County, Calif., only 20 years later. Jefferson County officials met Friday with U.S. government and Federal Reserve representatives in trying to avert a potential bankruptcy.

Jefferson is the largest county by population in Alabama. It has, however, been caught in a financial squeeze from collapsing bond markets and poor money management. In addition, the county's own debt has been shunned by investors due to turmoil in the municipal markets.

A similar jolt occurred to the municipal landscape in the early 1990s with Orange County. It is déjà vu, all over again. But this anything but funny (like Yogi Berra's slip of the tongue).

The costs of carrying debt related to a mammoth sewer project could alone reach $250 million for Jefferson County. To avoid bankruptcy, county officials will attempt to restructure some bonds and renegotiate payments. Raising taxes is also a consideration.

You have to wonder if this could happen in other counties or cities -- if it can happen in an area incorporating Birmingham, a quasi-banking capital. If there is a lesson to learn, it is for government agencies to practice fiscal restraint and minimize debt, especially as a possible recession looms.

Here in Nassau County, there are rumors of organizing a $140 million bond issue to pay for widening Highway A1A in Yulee. The premise was that the county would borrow the money to fund the overdue project now, and be repaid by the state later.

Within the city of Fernandina Beach, there have been discussions about borrowing money (by issuing bonds) to buy the downtown post office building, as well as an old church structure. Both these actions would result in multi-million-dollar bond issues during a time when the financial markets are tense and skittish. And municipal debt is being received as well as news reports from the Iraq War.

A bond issue is a financial tool for municipalities to borrow money. With unreceptive markets, a municipality will have to pay higher interest rates to try to attract buyers. In addition, the municipal markets are reeling due to the financial troubles of insurers that guarantee the principal on the AAA-rated bonds (it is unlikely that either Nassau County or Fernandina Beach would receive a triple-A rating, which is the highest).

In addition, municipalities in Florida have been dealt a blow by the implosion of a state-managed money fund. Withdrawals by cities and counties from the state fund have been restricted due to problems with sub-prime securities purchased by the managers.

To further complicate matters, the state -- and voters -- has mandated that cities and counties in Florida reduce their tax rates this year and in coming years.

Orange County became an infamous household name back in 1994 with its financial troubles. The size and scope of the Jefferson County problems are bigger than even those of Orange County.

This is not something you want to be known by.

A Fourth of July /July 2007

Since it is the 4th of July, it is fitting to talk about independence -- of our great country, and of our lives as Americans.

But what about financial independence? This is especially relevant for those who are close to retirement, or who have recently retired. Retirement is one of life's biggest deadlines, often termed the longest vacation you'll ever take.

If you have not noticed, Amelia Island, Yulee and the west side are quickly becoming retirement destinations. Our economy has flourished from the stream of retirees moving in from other states. They buy houses, goods, and services.

In other ways, retirees contribute to our community through volunteering, filling part-time jobs, or serving on non-profit boards. It is all part of making retirement enjoyable and fulfilling.

For some, retirement can be a challenge. Even wealthy retirees have fears of outliving their money. But you can be frugal during your retirement years.

It does not mean to have less fun, but be creative in choosing your leisure activities. You can play golf at the municipal course rather than at a high-dollar private resort, or clip a coupon and play for a discounted rate. If you like golf that much, get a job at a golf course -- and play for free.

Many retirees are taking on part-time jobs. Since people are retiring sooner and living longer these days, a part-time job as a crossing guard or as an artist or as a clerk can help fill in the financial gaps.

Then there is Social Security and Medicare. For most retirees, a full Social Security benefit is available at age 65 (you can take it as early as age 62). This is a pension we have each contributed to while working. And Medicare helps relieve the burden of high medical costs during retirement years, beginning at age 65.

According to a study by the Employee Benefit Research Institute, nearly two-thirds of workers age 55 and older have less than $100,000 saved for retirement. And half of current retirees have less than $50,000 to last them the rest of their lives.

But somehow they get by. They adjust their lifestyles. Some must tap into the value of what is often their biggest asset: their home. You can downsize to a smaller, less-expensive home in a lower-cost area.

Others are staying in their homes, and using home-equity lines of credit or reverse mortgages. These options must be used with caution, however.

The best news for retirees is this: You don't need as much income during retirement as you did while working. A common rule is that you need to replace about 70 percent of pre-retirement income to live the same lifestyle during retirement.

If you're still working, and can't seem to make the numbers work, why not work longer. Or settle for a second career (many local second-career retirees get into real estate, for instance.)

In this way, you can wait to take Social Security benefits, or some other pension. After all, you receive more if you wait.

Waiting. This can be a retirement strategy also.

Moving in, Moving out /May 2010

Caught in a riptide of excessive taxes, onerous regulations and heightened political demands, U.S. companies are steadily moving operations overseas to stay afloat.

The expenses of operating in the U.S. have become burdensome. Some companies are relocating their headquarters to foreign destinations; others are moving parts of their operations, such as manufacturing.

With each move, jobs often go with them.
U.S. officials seem oblivious to such trends. They often respond punitively by trying to attach penalties or taxes to such maneuvers. The tide of overseas operations is difficult to contain, however.

Financial behemoth J.P. Morgan is the latest corporation eyeballing a move overseas. The banking giant is looking to build a major corporate office in London to house its European operations.

Other intentions for the lavish facility, consisting of dual skyscrapers, are unclear at the moment.

Oil driller Transocean left the confines of the U.S. several years ago to relocate in Switzerland. Ironically, it is a Transocean rig - operated by British Petroleum (also foreign) - that recently ruptured in the Gulf of Mexico. The oil leak there has been ongoing for more than a month and has endangered marine life, birds and the livelihoods of many area businesses.

Other companies that have moved their headquarters overseas are similarly famous or infamous: Halliburton (previously run by former Vice President Dick Cheney), Accenture, Foster Wheeler, Ingersoll Rand, Tyco, Cooper Industries and Noble Drilling Services.

Some of the overseas pursuits are born out of a search for cheaper labor. Other reasons are to evade excessive U.S. taxes or to escape the grasp of pesky lawmakers looking for a fight. Either way, many more companies may ride the wave of foreign riches.

While some major companies are relocating outside the U.S., a spate of retail businesses has opened recently in downtown Fernandina Beach.

The openings are especially noteworthy within a treacherous economic environment that has forced many businesses to close their doors. Around the area, many retail spaces remain empty.

But not so in downtown Fernandina Beach. Even the seasonably slower winter months did not wreak as much havoc as normal in downtown. Few, if any, stores closed this off-season.

In addition, restaurants such as Kelley's Courtyard Cafe and Merge have opened while bars such as Indigo Alley expanded and thrived. Although not as recent, Café Karibo expanded and opened an adjoining microbrewery, Café Karibrew. And the former Bank of America building on Centre Street is being renovated in a major undertaking.

The reception of all these businesses has been exceptional. You have to respect entrepreneurs who embark on such ventures during difficult times.

They are opportune and bold, and can often ride the wave of prosperity when it returns to shore.

Technology has many other useful applications. Take the local website www.ameliaislandeasysearch.com.

The brainchild of ever-innovative Merritt Carlton, the website provides insightful statistics on the local property market. Carlton and real estate partner Sara Day intend for it to reveal trends and opportunities in the house and condominium markets here.

The colorful, appealing site provides statistics, opinions, and property listings locally and nationally. Want to know how many houses sold in the $250,000 to $500,000 price range in the last month? Look no further than here.

In fact, there are numerous deductions you can make from pouring over the statistics. Activity in the $250,000-and-under classification has been remarkably steady over the last four years – which includes one of the worst real estate downturns in the modern era.

However, higher-end houses and condos have felt the wrath of recession. Sales in the $250,000 to $749,000 class are about one-third of what they were in 2006.

But sales of properties priced $750,000 and higher have slowed to an agonizing crawl. Many of these are used as second homes or retirement relocations. The reason is simple why these higher-priced sales have declined.

Potential buyers have not been able to sell their properties in Connecticut, New Jersey and Pennsylvania, for instance – to then buy here. The markets in the northeast have also seized up in the downturn.

There is a silver lining, however. Sales are occurring – in all price ranges. Carlton has a realistically positive takeaway.

"It's starting to improve," Carlton says. "Things are doing better now."

Another Mouth to Feed   /March 1997

Some things never change, like the joy of a baby's birth.

But there is more to this basic equation of life today than simply assisting the human race to exist and multiply - there are multiplying costs. Raising this bundle of joy will cost you a bundle of cash.

Hefty costs of almost $250,000 will be tallied in raising each child. This includes typical expenses such as diapers and braces and summer camps. But these figures through the U.S. Department of Agriculture do not even include the staggering costs of college.

The USDA compiles the statistics through quarterly interviews with 5,000 families. The costs of raising a child are tracked only through age 17. If college costs are including another $20,000 to $150,000 must be added to the bill.

But there is a footnote of hope for those parents gasping for air. Many of the expenses are not really seen or felt. They are simply a part of everyday life, such as providing shelter for your child.

However, they are costs nonetheless. And lower-income families will not spend as much raising their children. The $250,000 figure is derived from a child in a family earning more than $65,000 a year.

Families earning less may spend as little as $120,000 - because private schools may not be an option, or you may eat Hamburger Helper for dinner instead of shrimp and linguine. The costs are broken down into seven categories: housing, food transportation, clothing, health care, childcare/education, and miscellaneous.

Housing is the biggest expense, but one that is hardest to determine. A formula is used by the USDA. It figures that 100 to 150 square feet of living space will be added per each child to a typical house.

A frugal parent might not add extra space, and instead let his four raucous children share a room (see health care costs). You could also move to an area where housing costs are lower. A more realistic compromise might be refinancing your debt.

In fact, housing translates into a third of the costs of raising a child. The more expensive a house the parents live in, the more expense computed per child. Again, the costs here are difficult to determine, as many large families cannot provide a separate room - or additional space - for each child.

To no surprise, the second biggest expense is food. It starts out with milk products in bottles and progresses to five ham-and-cheese sandwiches per lunch for that growing teenage boy. Aside from outright starvation techniques, there is not much you can do here.

You can buy items on sale and in bulk, particularly those you use on a weekly basis. But then you probably need extra space to store them. Wholesale clubs and web-based grocery sites might help you save on the bills.

Transportation, child care/education, and miscellaneous are the next costliest. Transportation entails the costs of a family car to transport the children, as well as buying a convertible for your 16-year old daughter. Childcare and education can vary in costs dramatically, especially if you opt for a private grade school or high school. Health care is also a big variable.

Miscellaneous includes everything that does not fit into these other categories, such as entertainment, reading materials and personal care items.

The least expensive is clothing, since the technique of "hand-me-downs" has prevailed through the ages. The popularity of second-hand shops, particularly in children's clothing, can also save money.

Altogether, these costs can prove substantial. The old days of having a big family to help with the farm are mostly over. Come to think of it, some things do change.

We're Still the Champ   /August 2007

Like a resilient and battle-tested pugilist, the Sunshine State is not ready to be counted out.

While some believe a confluence of expensive properties, runaway insurance costs, and spiraling taxes will undue Florida's steady growth, the statistics prove otherwise.

In fact, Florida has been growing twice as fast as the U.S. overall. From 2000 to 2006, the population in Florida has increased more than 13 percent, according to census figures. Florida residents grew in numbers from 16 million in 2000 to more than 18 million in 2006.

It is staggering to break down the population growth in the last six years. It adds up to about 330,000 people per year moving to Florida, or 6,400 people a week. Or about 900 people per day. Meanwhile, the population growth in the U.S. has been about 6 percent among all of the 3,141 counties. So there clearly is no cause for even a standing-eight count for Florida.

In Nassau County, the population is 66,707 as of the latest tally -- a 15 percent increase from 2000. Nassau is 40th largest of the 67 counties in Florida.

Nearby Flagler County has dwarfed the growth here, however. And anywhere else, for that matter. Flagler's population has grown by more than 66 percent from 2000 to 2006 (to 83,000 residents). It ranks as the nation's fastest-growing county. The explosive community of Palm Coast is the biggest draw there.

There are similarities between Flagler (just north of Daytona Beach) and Nassau counties. Both are coastal communities along the U.S. I-95 corridor, attractive retirement locations, and offer a lot of land for growth.

According to the 2006 census, Nassau County has 102 people per square mile. In plain arithmetic, that would mean there are 653 square miles here, stretching from Amelia Island westward to Callahan, Hilliard and Bryceville.

The average people-per-square-mile figure within the counties of Florida is 337. This means Nassau is one-third as populated as the average county in the state (this obviously equates to more room for growth).

In comparison, Miami-Dade is the most populated county with 2.4 million residents and 1,271 people per square mile. The largest county in North Florida is Duval, with 830,000 residents and 1,100 people per square mile. Duval's county seat is Jacksonville.

In comparison to other states, Florida is about to take third place in population from New York. Much of Florida's growth has come at New York's expense. For instance, between 1995 and 2000, more than 300,000 people moved from New York to Florida -- the largest state-to-state flow in the U.S. during that time.

Florida's growth has allowed it to capture seats in the U.S. House of Representatives. Florida is expected to tie or overtake New York in the number of congressional seats, which brings with it political clout.

So Florida's growth may have slowed of late, due mostly to a weakened real-estate market. But this champion of growth is not yet dethroned.

Waiting on the Trumpet Call   /June 2007

All we need now is for some national magazine to pronounce that the real estate market is dead.

In past economic and market declines, a major magazine's pronouncement of this nature has often signaled the bottom. The magazine's cover page would likely show rows of "For Sale" signs that look like picket fences and some startling headline about the death of real estate in the U.S.

It might be on a local magazine rack next week.

To put salt on a wound, mortgage-lending criteria has reportedly been tightened due to bankruptcies and foreclosures and worthless sub-prime loans. The ramifications have been felt throughout the global credit markets.

Here, on Amelia Island and in the rest of Nassau County, it has been insulated in the past from national downturns in real estate. The real estate market here has always been steady and predictable.

That changed about 10 years ago. Real estate values here and elsewhere in Florida increased like the mosquito population after a rain. Oceanfront properties doubled in value, and in some case, tripled. There was a rampage to buy, regardless of price or location.

Local experts say things have changed over the past year or two. Bidding wars over properties have been replaced by sales delays -- sometimes, months long. But it is almost to be expected, following the momentous run-up in prices.

Bobby Ferreira has seen numerous downturns in the real estate market during his 30 years with Century 21 John T. Ferreira & Son, Inc. Ferreira, who owns the local agency, says this is the fourth slow market he's seen in real estate.

"In two short years, we have gone from a booming market with many buyers vying for a limited number of properties," Ferreira says, "to the current market of a large inventory of unsold properties."

The evidence is in the pudding. The Multiple Listing Service utilized by real-estate agents has increased in size from 750 properties for sale in 2005 to more than 2,000 listings today.

Ferreira and other veterans see this as the "cyclical nature" of real estate.

However, something is different this time. In the past, downturns have been precipitated by higher interest rates, or inflation, or recession. The economy in the U.S. is strong right now, interest rates are low by historical standards, and the global marketplace is booming.

Ferreira believes the extreme appreciation of prior years is the culprit locally. The demand here could not keep up with the escalating prices. Also, high property taxes and insurance costs have hindered the market.

Dee Chaplin, who along with Hugh Williams owns the Chaplin Williams Real Estate office locally, feels the earlier run-up in prices here was part of an adjustment.

"Our higher prices needed to happen," Chaplain says, "because we were the cheapest place by far on the eastern seaboard."

The following slowdown in the real estate market is normal. "This is a typical real estate market," Chaplain says. "It's cyclical. It goes up and down."

At some point, it's going to be a great time to buy. There always is an opportunistic entry point after a slowdown. The only problem is that no one rings a bell when prices have bottomed.

The trumpet call from that magazine is the first sign, however.

The Fallout from Katrina   /April 2007

Hurricane Katrina battered the Gulf Coast two long years ago, but aftershocks are still being felt.

High-dollar lawsuits abound in class-action status. Blue tarps still identify patched-up rooftops. Some small towns, especially in rural Mississippi and Alabama, are not rebuilt.

But repercussions are felt as far away as here. If you haven't noticed, finding adequate property/homeowners' insurance is sort of like uncovering a shark's tooth on the beach. You have to do a lot of sifting.

Some insurance companies have ceased issuing homeowners' policies in Florida and in other states bordering the Gulf of Mexico, perceiving it as too risky. You would have received a non-renewal notice if this applied to you.

While other insurance can be found, rates are higher by thousands of dollars for some local residents. If you own a condominium, second home, or rental property, the search for coverage can be even more trying.

And there is always the risk that you are not properly insured. Many of the lawsuits stemming from Katrina-based losses reportedly had to do with policies written incorrectly or fictitiously. Some homeowners, in an attempt to secure a lower-cost policy, may fabricate information in the underwriting process.

The policy is then issued based upon the false information about their property -- but is often not worth the paper it is written on. In other instances (from personal experiences), policies are written incorrectly by insurance agencies themselves, through a pursuit of new business or through sloppiness.

There are instances of two-story houses being insured as one-story residences. In other cases, insurance is titled incorrectly. For instance, a rental property is titled to a limited-liability corporation, but the insurance is issued in the individual owner's name. This can cause a claim to be denied.

Property insurance is not the only area that could be problematic. Flood insurance falls under the same scrutiny. Flood insurance is subsidized by the federal government -- and normally insures up to $250,000 of value. Excess flood insurance policies can often be obtained through private or public insurers.

Sometimes, a debate arises over whether the damage to a property resulted from rising water (flood) or high winds (hurricane). This has been known to delay the payment of homeowners' claims.

In Florida, Citizens Insurance is a state-funded program for high-risk properties. These are normally properties that cannot be insured by private insurance companies. So the state insures them.

However, Citizens coverage is inferior in many regards. It is costly and often does not cover all the needs of a property owner. Even though it may be inadequate, it sometimes is the only option. In conclusion, find a reputable insurance agent and get an insurance check-up. Don't wait until a problem occurs.

Make sure your insurance is properly written and adequate to replace your property in event of a loss. Too little coverage is almost as bad as none at all. And make sure it is written correctly, with updated and accurate information.

This is truly one situation where it pays to be proactive, not reactive. Katrina and her predecessors proved that.

Greener Pastures for Retirees   /July 2007

For Florida retirees, the grass may be greener elsewhere --
particularly in other southern states.

Retirees once attracted to Florida for reasonable housing
prices, a lack of a state income tax, and steady sunshine are now
looking elsewhere. It is a matter of searching for greener pastures.

Sky-high property taxes and insurance costs are pushing
away retirees on fixed, or somewhat fixed, incomes. Just across the
border, in places like Georgia and Alabama, property taxes and
insurance are significantly less.

Consider these two real-life examples:

-- A soon-to-be retiree from South Florida was looking to
sell his $1.2 million house and move to North Florida. He wanted
to find a quiet, idyllic location with an ocean outlet along the St.
Johns River for his sailboat. It appeared to make for a peaceful
retirement.

He planned to use the equity from his house in Coconut
Grove to purchase the new place for cash. No mortgage
payment would bring retirement bliss. However, a comparably
priced home in the $1 million range in North Florida would bring
with it a tax bill of about $2,000 per month, or $24,000 per year.

The tax bill alone would be like having a substantial
mortgage payment. And that doesn't even include property
insurance.

Across the border, in northern Alabama on a picturesque
lake, he instead found a place for about the same price -- $950,000.
He could still get to the Gulf of Mexico along the inland waterway.
True retirement bliss, once again. But the new property tax bill:
about $200 per month.

-- Another soon-to-be retiree is looking to build a house in
the North Georgia mountains. He bought a parcel on a
mountainside overlooking a lake. In trying to decide where to move
when he retires, he is comparing the Georgia mountain home with
an oceanfront condominium in St. Augustine he also owns.

The decision is easy. In this town in Georgia, property is
appraised at 40 percent of its current value; you pay taxes at this
reduced amount. The tax bill would therefore be substantially less

for him in Georgia -- than in Florida. (Georgia has a state income tax, which Florida does not.)

It is not just so-called "wealthy" people who are feeling the tax bite. Someone who buys a lower-priced house on Amelia Island or Yulee right now, for instance, could still be looking at a tax bill of about $5,000 a year. That's more than $400 per month in taxes alone. Insurance costs on the same house would be $200 per month.

The costs are now forcing people away. Neighboring states in the Sun Belt are competing for retirees' money also. Georgia, the Carolinas, as well as Alabama have become prime retirement destinations. The weather is about the same as Florida, with substantially lower housing costs.

A lasting loss of retirees' money could be devastating for Florida. The real-estate market -- a major driver of the economy here -- would inevitably cool even more. The demand for real estate would slacken, driving down prices. The same positive effect on real-estate prices from retirees' purchases would work in the reverse.

And the impact on real estate of the newer retirees, the Baby Boomers, should continue for another 20 or 30 years. That is a long time for someone, or some state, to benefit from this new wave of Baby Boomers-turned-retirees.

Florida's Public Schools Improve /August 2007

Move over California, New York and Minnesota. Make room, because Florida's public schools are moving to the head of the class.

In a list of the 1,200 top public schools in the U.S. just published by <u>Newsweek,</u> Florida schools truly dominated the rankings. Of the top 50 schools, 12 are in Florida. From the top 100, an impressive 22 are Florida schools. No other state was close.

But there was even more startling news. Coming in a little farther down the list, at No. 1,022, is Fernandina Beach High School. And who said Florida's public schools were trailing their national counterparts?

The formula used for the list looked at the number of graduating seniors at each school in the country. The graduates were graded by the number of them taking advanced placement classes, or taking the prestigious International Baccalaureate or Cambridge tests.

The 1,200 schools in the list are among the top five percent of schools nationally (using this formula). In addition to Fernandina Beach High appearing on the list, there were numerous others from North Florida.

The highest-ranking area school was Stanton College Prep in Jacksonville at No. 3 in the nation. Others were Paxon School for Advanced Studies at No. 15; Nease at No. 78; Anderson School of the Arts at No. 364; Bartram Trail at No. 455; and Mandarin at No. 777.

Premier private schools in the area such as Bolles, Bishop Kinney and Episcopal are not included in the list. Private schools would naturally have a higher ratio, since many of those students are taking advanced placement courses as well as higher-level tests.

Florida's dominance is surprising. State legislators pushed through the new Florida Comprehensive Assessment Test (FCAT) in recent years because of lagging national comparisons and somewhat of a stigma here. The tests are intended to provide a standard yardstick to measure the academic performance of Florida students versus their peers.

A similar level of lofty criteria is used in the <u>Newsweek</u> rankings. Schools are often measured by the best students they produce. Top students often qualify for advanced placement classes, and pursue premier levels of testing in efforts to be recognized by the best colleges.

Texas and New York are the two other states that ranked highly. Texas took six of the top 50 spots, with Talented and Gifted school as No. 1 in the nation and Science/Engineering Magnet school ranking as No. 2. Both are in Dallas.

New York had eight schools in the top 50. The oft-heralded schools in California and Minnesota did not rank as highly as expected. In contrast, Florida schools flourished in the list, particularly in the top 100 places.

It appears that the so-called "newer" states -- with state-of-the-art schools and plenty of funding -- ranked the highest, in comparison to older Northeastern schools, for instance. Of course, Florida, Texas and New York are three of the largest states by population.

But that certainly does not take away from the performance of Florida's schools. And for tiny Fernandina Beach High to meet such a high standard is a feather in teachers' caps there.

Our hats are off to you -- and the scholars you are producing.

Restoring Vigor to Real Estate   /March 2007

Mired in a slump, Florida real estate could jump with vigor under state-proposed tax reforms.

Proposals to mandate lower property taxes around the state could infuse life and activity into real estate here. Cumbersome property taxes as well as spiraling insurance costs are slowing real-estate transactions and hurting values here.

State lawmakers are charging ahead with sweeping tax reforms. One proposal calls for property tax rates in cities and counties to be reduced to 2001 levels -- with limited increases from there.

If some version of tax reform is approved, county and city governments in the state would have to overhaul and streamline operations. Local governments would essentially have to operate on fewer funds.

The state homestead exemption that residents covet is designed to limit the size of local governments. However, local governments have found other sources of tax revenues.

For instance, taxes have been levied inequitably on businesses and investment properties. Since taxes can only be raised incrementally on homesteaded properties, local governments have placed the burden elsewhere.

Overall, property taxes around the state have escalated sharply. This could eventually hinder the state's economy, in tandem with exorbitant homeowners' insurance costs.

The property tax rate in Nassau County is moderate in relation to other equally-sized counties in Florida. Nonetheless, the taxes on businesses and investment properties are higher here than in many other parts of the country.

This is partially due to a substantial run-up in values over recent years, as well as the tax burden being placed firmly upon businesses, non-homesteaded properties, and new construction. State lawmakers are aware of this, and have pledged to address it in their current session.

Another popular proposal would permit homeowners to take their exemptions with them upon selling. Lawmakers contend that many residents are trapped in their homes, since they would lose their reduced tax valuations upon selling and buying elsewhere in Florida.

State lawmakers have been busy. In addition to tax reforms, they have already taken action to defray homeowners' insurance costs. Gov. Charlie Crist signed a bill in January that promises rate cuts.

The bill reportedly will reduce insurance rates -- particularly for wind coverage pertaining to hurricanes -- by 10 to 50 percent. Most of the reductions will be seen in South Florida, where insurance costs are highest in the state.

Meanwhile, local governments are scrambling to assess the impact if tax reforms are passed. Nassau County would reportedly lose about $25 million in property tax revenues under current proposals. The impact would be minimal in Fernandina Beach -- due to commendable attempts by city commissioners to roll back the property tax rate each year.

Any tax reforms are still a long way from becoming law. There are discussions about getting reform measures on a ballot (for voters' approval) by later this year.

Either way, reforms are coming – doused with economic vigor.

Planning for the Boom   /May 2007

North Florida is a place on the move.

Population in the counties of Baker, Clay, Duval, Nassau, Putnam and St. Johns is expected to more than double in coming years. It is the continuation of a growth boom that is consuming the entire state.

Around the state, the population is expected to double to 18 million residents by 2060. This equates to 900 new people moving here each day. Flagler and Baker counties are among eight rural areas projected to undergo the most radical changes over that time.

To accommodate the growth, some seven million acres of agriculture and other rural land will be developed in the future into urban settings across the state. The startling process has already occurred in some areas.

The urban build-out is expected to peak in the hub of North Florida, Duval County, by the year 2040. From there, it will continue to spill into Nassau, Clay, St. Johns and Baker counties.

In Nassau County, the population is projected to reach 150,000 in the next 50 years. There are currently 66,000 residents now. The projections are from a study by a growth-management group, 1000 Friends of Florida.

Nassau officials are meeting regularly to hammer out codes and covenants for growth. They hope to have a handbook of sorts that will spell out what is allowed and what is not.

A big problem is that the book is still not complete. Therefore, the explosion in population in past years has largely gone unregulated. It is plain to the eye to see.

Already in St. Johns County, an estimated 70,000 to 120,000 new homes have been approved to be built. The discrepancy in those numbers caused a housecleaning of county commissioners there. It apparently demonstrated a lack of control and oversight.

The projected number for new homes for Nassau is closer to 10,000, although several gargantuan projects -- such as those on the Rayonier land both east and west of U.S. Interstate 95 – could cause that number to soar.

Much of Amelia Island and Fernandina Beach are already built out. Unless existing houses and commercial buildings are razed, the ability for new development on the island is limited.

The transformation from rural areas to urban settings is going on before our eyes. It is hitting close to home, with wildfire-like development along State Highway A1A -- in Yulee and now onto Callahan.

Everyone knows the wave of new residents is coming. Few states, if any, will grow as rapidly as Florida in coming years. The Sunshine State is having its day in the sun.

For local officials, a big task is at hand. Plan now -- or forever regret it.

An Adventurous Retirement Plan /May 2008

Kit Cooper had something a little more adventurous in mind for her retirement.

As a Fernandina Beach resident, Cooper had already experienced the quiet, seaside-escape routine. She worked in the real-estate industry here until a few years ago, when she headed out on a business venture that segued into retirement.

She now owns a private residence with servants' quarters and mountain vistas overlooking an ancient volcanic crater filled with spring water. It is her slice of paradise, Nicaraguan-style. Cooper is not the only local resident with ties to Nicaragua.

For one, a local mortgage broker she knows has bought into the Nicaraguan story of retirement nirvana. Low costs, suitable health care, and affordable property all add up to a retirement destination viewed by many as the next Costa Rica.

MSNBC has featured Nicaragua as one of "The Best-Kept Retirement Secrets," and U.S. News & World Report identified it as one of the top ten retirement destinations in the world. However, there are some drawbacks to life in a Central American country.

"It's not for the faint of heart," Cooper says. There is an element of the "Wild West" to the Nicaraguan lifestyle. Crime (mostly thefts), pollution, and limited amenities can present obstacles to tourists and retirees alike. If you can stomach some of the non-western attributes, it's a pretty palatable place by Cooper's standards.

There are even government benefits afforded to foreign retirees in Nicaragua, similar to those offered by Costa Rica in the 1980s. These mostly involve tax incentives for foreigners.

Under certain circumstances, a foreign retiree will not pay taxes on out-of-country earnings and can bring in some Nicaragua household goods and automobiles without being taxed. You can also own property there and still be a citizen of the U.S. (as long as you leave the country every 90 days).

Real estate prices are commonly 20 to 60 percent less than in the U.S. Taxes are ridiculously low, and property insurance is negligible. For instance, a $200,000 property at Laguna de Apoyo (near where Cooper lives) would entail the following monthly costs: $200 for utilities, $100 for a full-time maid, $75 for cable and phone, $50 for health insurance, and $200 for groceries.

Health-care standards increased dramatically with the opening of the state-of-the-art Vivian Pellas Metropolitan Hospital in Managua. The city of more than one million people also has other health-care offerings that rival those in the western world.

The costs of healthcare are eye-opening: $45 for a physician's house call, $17 for an x-ray, less than $75 for an emergency room visit, and $100 for a hospital bed for a night. The final retirement straw for Cooper is her house, nestled in a two-acre compound with walls around it and a view that spans the mountains, the lake, and neighboring cities and waterways.

It's a view "that would cost me $3 million here (in Florida) -- if I could find it," Cooper says.

Ducking a 1-2-3 Combination   /January 2004

As the U.S. economy struggles to its feet after being blindsided by a one-two-three combination of terrorism, a slumping stock market and a turbulent war, Nassau County has hardly broken a sweat.

In fact, the only sweat associated with this area has been that of elected officials trying to figure out how to cope with the growth -- and of builders trying to keep up with the demand. In our microcosm of the world, things are good economically.

You can see it everywhere you look. Shopping plazas and subdivisions and road projects are springing up across the county. Even on the rural west side, a new business plaza in Hilliard is almost filled with tenants, and in Callahan, available retail space is scarce.

Businesses looking for space in Callahan have to move quickly when something suitable becomes available. The growth on Amelia Island has washed over into Yulee like a hurricane-spawned wave hitting the beach. Wooded parcels are being converted into upscale golf-course communities like North Hampton, with another neighboring community planned there.

You can see growth spreading like a California wildfire along the Highway A1A corridor, through Yulee, jumping across U.S. I-95 and on to Callahan along the section of road soon to be four lanes.

Already, there are reports of subdivisions planned for the A1A section west of I-95. While conservationists scrutinize their every move, developers are searching out any vacant parcels for future projects.

Meanwhile, many regions of the U.S. are not as fortunate. The financial districts of some major cities have been vacated as businesses try to decentralize in the new world infiltrated by terrorists. Also, the economic recession and the worst stock market probably since the Great Depression have forced many businesses to downsize.

Some towns as near as St. Marys have had to try to cope with major industries shutting their doors and moving elsewhere -- particularly to overseas markets where unions are non-existent and labor is cheap. State and municipal governments yearn for operating funds in less-appealing areas where more people and businesses are moving out than moving in. This often results in a reduction in public services.

The fallout from the dot-com bubble can still be felt in areas such as Silicon Valley as well as in upscale places where the dot-com billionaires -- who are now millionaires -- built houses and lavish buildings.

But Nassau County has emerged with shining colors. Now that things seem to be improving in the economic sense across the country, an even brighter future for this area lies over the horizon.

As the population here continues to grow -- fed by businesspeople wanting an idyllic lifestyle with access to an airport, by retirees seeking out warm weather and peace and quiet, and the ultra-wealthy buying a lavish second or third home -- the Lowe's and Super Wal-Mart and Applebee's stores will continue to come.

Growth comes with a price tag, indeed. But the price you pay normally is pennies in regard to the riches an area receives.

Tennis Tournament Served Us Well   /July 2008

With the speed of a Maria Sharapova serve, Amelia Island may soon lose some of its global panache.

The women's professional tennis tournament, held here each spring for 29 years, may be moving down the road. The former Bausch & Lomb Championships tournament has brought global recognition and exposure to Amelia Island.

It is unfortunate that the tournament may be moved next year to the Sawgrass Country Club in Ponte Vedra Beach. Over the years, the tournament has attracted famous players like Martina Navratilova, Chris Everett, and recently, Sharapova herself.

The move has very much to do with sponsorships. Bausch & Lomb had announced that it would no longer sponsor the event for undisclosed reasons. That put local organizers on notice to find a new main sponsor -- and keep the tournament here, at the Amelia Island Plantation.

Tournament officials are reportedly close to signing the contract to relocate the event to Ponte Vedra Beach. The tournament will fit nicely for that town as another major sporting event to complement The Players Championship golf tournament, held there each spring.

The tennis tournament has completed a dynamic springtime lineup for Amelia Island. It fit comfortably between two other favorite events -- the Concours d'Elegance in March and the Eight Flags Shrimp Festival in May.

The tournament has been televised by ESPN for some time now. Television cameras have a way of delivering an intimate portrayal of an area. You can still hear the announcer's voice resonate the words "here on beautiful Amelia Island" as local scenes flickered across the screen.

There was a debate over how much the tournament contributed to the island's economy. Some retailers have said they saw little increase in shopping activity that weekend, although there was no denying the popularity and appeal of the event.

Many of the spectators drove in and drove out after each day's matches. Others stayed within the cozy confines of the Plantation. But local tourism officials are correct in labeling the

Bausch & Lomb Championships a "signature event." An area is fortunate to have such events to draw attention and tourism.

As with the rest of the state, a major driver of the economy here is tourism. Putting the area under the microscope of TV cameras for a weekend of tennis (the tournament actually lasted most of a week) is irreplaceable. The benefits, and the exposure, will not be easily replaced by something else.

And, to complicate matters, there are preliminary reports that the widely renowned Concours car show is being solicited by other towns. Like with the tennis tournament, any temptation for an event to leave our area should be mitigated before it becomes a reality.

Our little slice of paradise has so much to offer. Getting opportunities to show it off are few. Let's not put our community in this type of predicament again.

Focus our efforts and attention on "signature" events and activities such as these. Quibbling over minor affairs -- as we often do -- does nothing to benefit our community.

Many of our local businesses and residents rely on tourism for their livelihoods. In addition, it is a clean industry that keeps on giving -- as in giving back, not giving away.

Part Four: Society

A Pick-Me-Up /July 2007

We had played pick-up basketball with the middle-aged man a few times. He had a slim, chiseled build, with sandy-blond hair and an unabashed passion for life. And surprising spring in his jump shot for someone his age.

He worked for a large restaurant in South Jacksonville, as a manager. But a call for duty, to serve and support his country, led him away to Iraq when the conflict there started. He seemed driven by the similar patriotism as NFL football player Pat Tilman.

Just last week, he climbed out of the car next to me. His voice was hoarse and gurgled. He blurted out with the same fervor that he would be back to play basketball with us -- once he got his hip replaced.

I inquired about his hip injury. Was it a sports injury from his active lifestyle?

No, it wasn't from anything that had to do with exercise -- or the bounce of a ball. It had to do with his body bouncing off the ground and through the air, propelled by the blast of an incoming missile from the mysterious enemy in Iraq.

He showed a scar down his throat, and one along his belly. He said he was lucky to be alive. He did not hear this missile coming, from his location inside one of the corridors of horror in Iraq. He only remembers waking up three weeks later in Shands Hospital.

Once he gets his new hip, he is eventually heading back to Iraq. He is a supervisor in his civilian support role, and they need him there. He became somber when I asked if things were improving in Iraq. It's interesting to hear the inside story from someone who has been there and who has no agenda.

He shook his head, his eyes searching. You could hear him inhale through his revamped throat. "No," he whispered, like a warrior having to admit defeat. He then limped away.

Thirsting for Inspiration   /August 2010

We have had a drought of precipitation in North Florida in recent months.

We've also experienced an agonizing drought of inspiration – here and elsewhere.

Wherever you turn, negative thoughts and reports and inferences smack you in the face with a sobering slap. Any encouragement or hope is doused with the reality of enduring one of the most difficult recessions in our nation's history.

The BP oil spill. A sluggish real estate market. An economy staggering to its feet. Flash crashes. Woes from the Euro zone. The highest unemployment seen in the U.S. since the early 1980s.

The litany of hopelessness goes on and on.

Several local churches here have embraced the reality of today – and attempted to brighten it. Religion is a big industry in the U.S. and the world. Look no farther than the Roman Catholic Church, with a billion members and immeasurably global clout.

The Journey Church is relatively new to Fernandina Beach, but like other churches here has grown and sprouted with a burgeoning membership. The church offers a modern service with a traditional message, accompanied by a band playing Christian music and big-screen monitors and bright lights.

In a detour from its traditional offerings this past weekend, the church brought in Vietnam veteran and inspirational speaker Tim Lee.

Lee has lived through dark, depressing times. All that he has experienced in his life is the loss of both legs from an explosion in a minefield. He was passed off as dead, even by fellow soldiers. But he recovered, and accepted his new condition. And now he wants to revive hope for everyone who listens to him.

He races around the country and the world in his wheelchair, his bold blue Marines uniform and his multi-colored metals, spreading the world of Christianity. He has built up an impressive practice within Tim Lee Ministries.

With rugged looks and square shoulders, he looks like a Marine – from his waist up. But the half of his body salvaged from the field in Vietnam is the most important part. He speaks forcefully, passionately, like a Marine officer.

The son of a pastor, he pursued sports and the normal transgressions as a teenager. He joined the Marines at a time when he felt his life was spiraling. He was clamoring for direction.

Until that fateful day, when he was filling the point position in a patrol. He insisted on leading his men during the minesweeping operation, eager to lead by example.

He still leads by example. He uses religion as a foundation, a framework, for leading a good, moral life. He does not regret his misfortunes. Instead, he views them as critical turning points in his life.

They have steered him toward the crusade he proudly and tirelessly carries on today. A crusade of hope and inspiration. We could use more of this message in today's fractured world.

Like the drought-stricken foliage here, we are thirsting for it.

Remain Calm after WTC Attack   /September 2001

(Editor's note: This article appeared in the Nassau County edition of the Florida Times-Union newspaper.)

As Americans congregated in front of televisions at home, work and in public places on Tuesday, it was unlikely their first thoughts had much to do with the many financial offices in New York's World Trade Center twin towers that were destroyed by two terrorist acts.

But later in the day, as the dust literally began to clear, speculation circulated about what the financial impacts would be to the United States and the world.

"The main thing people should remember is to stay calm and clear-headed," said Steve Nicklas, a financial adviser for Prudential and Fernandina Beach resident. "Panic is the worst thing to do, like the people who were calling Prudential (Tuesday) and saying they wanted to get rid of their portfolio and get out of investing. It's just hard to say how these current events will fall out."

An already unstable market has caused much concern to investors well before this week's tragedy, Nicklas said, but if consumers have not panicked yet about recent drops, they should not now because historical trends show trading rises, falls and then recovers.

"I hope people will remain calm because we've never really seen anything like this in the U.S.," said Nicklas, who nearly one year ago spent time in the Morgan Stanley Dean Witter offices of the World Trade Center in New York. "Historically the financial markets have been in place for more than 100 years and have seen and survived major public events that the markets have recovered from.

"They always have and they always will."

Oprah Searches for Love   /August 2011

When Oprah Winfrey's TV network went fishing for a pond to hold a new reality series, it got hooked on the tiny town of Kingsland, Ga. some time ago.

And the South Georgia town known for its annual Catfish Festival eventually landed the "Lovetown, USA" show, to be televised on Winfrey's OWN network. But it was not a lucky bite.

The townspeople of Kingsland put on their best performances when Winfrey's crews came calling in recent months. They dressed in red, decorated the town with ribbons, and hosted a block party to differentiate themselves from other towns vying for the spot.

Crews for the show will now spend the next 30 days in Kingsland, helping eight single residents find love. They will do it through match-making techniques -- and then follow the fledgling lovebirds through their courtships.

Oprah, who was in neighboring St. Marys, Ga. this weekend for a rally, will revisit Kingsland after the 30 days of dating to see what has transpired. The rally, held at the St. Marys' waterfront park, marked the official kickoff of the show.

Kingsland's 12,305 residents are obviously excited. The windfall from the production will inevitably benefit the town and its businesses, while providing entertainment for the residents.

The concept of finding love for residents is being deemed "the biggest dating challenge in TV history." Kingsland outshined other towns such as Carrboro, NC (nicknamed "the Paris of the Piedmont") and Natchez, Miss., where Disney filmed "The Adventures of Huck Finn."

The desired location appeared to be small towns with fewer than 15,000 residents. Not only is Winfrey trying to help townsfolk in Kingsland find love, she also wants to investigate the effects of widespread love "on the DNA of one American community."

The participants in the show can range from 20 to 60 years old. They must fill out a 20-page questionnaire that asks everything from religion to clothes size to favorite food.

The original series will premiere this summer, with eight episodes. The match-making efforts will certainly be in experienced hands. Paul Carrick, who is the real-life "Hitch" from the popular movie, will work with Kailen Rosenberg, who is known as the true "love whisperer" and has assisted in 200 successful marriages.

As with everything she does, Winfrey intends for this reality show to be different from the rest. That's just part of her own DNA.

"That's why I came down," Winfrey said, "to say that it's not just another reality show."

Can Shrimpers Stay Afloat?   /August 2007

What would it be like for the town proclaimed as the "Birthplace of the (Modern) Shrimping Industry" to no longer have shrimp boats that call it home?

It would be like St. Augustine calling itself "The Ancient City" -- with nothing but new construction. Or Jacksonville calling itself "The River City" and not having a river.

Fernandina Beach's heritage is as rich as a Saudi oil sheik. It also pronounces itself as the "Isle of Eight Flags," since the town has been ruled by eight different countries within its colorful past.

However, shrimping is what the town is associated with, and rightfully so. The annual "Shrimp Festival" attracts 100,000 people and boosts our visibility and economy each spring. The pink color and delectable taste of a shrimp from the Fernandina Beach waters is known far and wide.

Years ago, seafood processing plants dotted the Fernandina Beach waterfront. The shrimp boat fleet was large and impressive. The fishing, shrimping, and shellfish industry has been a staple here for many years.

The future of shrimp boats docking along the local waterfront is in a state of flux, however. Improving and invigorating the waterfront is important to our economy and to the businesses in historic downtown. Marinas and waterfronts can be a lifeline of tourism.

Hopefully, there will be provisions in the final plans to include docks for local shrimp boats. The powerful masts and seaworthy nets of the shrimp boats are a focal point of the marina. They have always been there, it seems.

There has been much discussion and compromise over the marina redevelopment. You must make the development profitable for the commercial side, but also appease the conservationists. There seems to have been an amicable give-and-take approach thus far.

The fleet of shrimp boats here has dwindled over the years. The shrimping industry has gone through a difficult time, beset with high fuel costs and competition from foreign imports of shrimp. However, it is not dead and gone.

Look no farther than Mayport. The docks there are lined with numerous shrimp boats. Several seafood processing plants fuel the local economy there. The seafood industry in Mayport appears to be bustling.

It has spilled over into other areas in Mayport. Like here, low-rise townhouses are being proposed for the waterfront, and there are rumors of a major cruise ship coming to the sleepy town. A gambling boat is already there.

As for Fernandina Beach, the days of seafood processing plants here are probably a thing of the past. But keeping the shrimpers here is not only an economical asset, but also a part of our tradition and lore. The shrimpers have been here a lot longer than most of us.

Locals recall the old days, when shrimp boats would race against each other as a highlight of the annual "Shrimp Festival." The festival reportedly celebrates the start of the shrimping season. Let's not bring to an end the shrimping industry here.

The downtown revitalization should include our fleet of shrimp boats, even if it must be placed at the city marina. There is plenty of waterfront to make room for them.

The town known as the birthplace of shrimping should not represent the death of it.

Grass Roots Are Sprouting   /October 2007

In case you haven't noticed, there is a grass-roots citizens' group growing down the road from you -- planting and spreading its seeds of influence.

More than ever, local residents are banding together through citizens' groups to oppose lousy government, unregulated growth, and any other issue that could rattle our precious slice of tranquility. There is certainly a litany of causes and issues.

But the strength and broadness of the community groups embody the biggest issues. It appears that residents have simply had enough. And they are acting through these emerging groups to deliver their unified views to local officials.

For instance, a proposed apartment building off Barnwell Road brought out more than 200 people to a county meeting. Most of the residents opposed the development due to increased traffic and congestion it would cause.

In another instance, a proposal to close county parks and beaches between sunset and sunrise drew 300 people to the commission chambers. People were standing outside the meeting room, in the hallway, and practically out the door.

Residents did not want to give up another one of their freedoms -- in this case, using the city parks and beaches whenever they please. In both cases, the residents won. Due to sheer numbers, probably. And resonating opinions.

The number of citizens' groups is increasing, as is the memberships. Several homeowners groups represent thousands of local residents, for instance.

The largest remaining of these groups, the East Nassau Homeowners' Council, has previously represented only associations off the island. The group, headed by Robert Weintraub, is now open to homeowners groups on Amelia Island.

The group prides itself in providing a voice for its members as well as serving as a conduit of information. When you combine several thousand residents into a powerful voting bloc, it seems their voices are heard more easily.

The Amelia Island Association, Inc. has restructured itself in recent months. The AIA previously represented homeowners groups on Amelia Island, but will now focus on and serve the homeowners themselves -- in neighborhoods, as well as in non-neighborhood settings.

It presents itself as "an association of residents and supporters" of Amelia Island, focusing on the quality of life here and the efficiency of local governments. It will inform members through its website and e-mailed AIA alerts.

Just down the island, the "Concerned Friends of Fernandina" is yet another grass-roots citizens group. Its focus is on the city of Fernandina Beach, but it tackles county problems also. Its slogan is to "inform and involve residents wanting to preserve the small town identity ... and natural beauty" of Fernandina Beach.

Longstanding groups such as the Sierra Club and other national organizations are also present here. They also have been pivotal in shaping local policies and decisions.

The Sierra Club boasts 1.3 million members and supporters across the country. It is the granddaddy of influential grass-roots organizations, with a bent toward the environment.

And to top it off, the seeds of grass-root groups here are being fertilized through savvy, intelligent, and committed members, such as Robert Weintraub and Phil Scanlon and Julie Ferreira and Eric Titcomb.

They are cultivating the issues -- to allow the seeds to grow.

Virginia Tech Massacre Miscues   /April 2007

What does it take to get kicked out of school these days?

Do the following acts constitute grounds for dismissal: intimidating teachers; disrupting classes; stalking fellow students; setting a fire in your dormitory; or being identified as a danger and ordered to visit a mental hospital?

How about when all these acts are committed by the same student in a short time? Murdering two students on a wintry April morning might get an administration's attention. But not even that was enough for school officials to intervene and likely prevent the massacre at Virginia Tech University.

And you wonder why many parents and students and impartial observers are ready to throw the book at the university president and the college's police chief. Universities are a big business these days. Their main business is to educate students -- and protect them while on campus.

A university is supposed to be a public sanctuary, free or intimidation, harassment, and danger. The tuitions are high enough and administrators are compensated enough to expect this. The money collected at the gates of college sporting events is enough to support this.

So what went wrong on the idyllic campus in Blacksburg, Virginia? If you listen to the excuses and alibis of school officials, the massacre was unavoidable and had nothing to do with their lack of action.

They contend they could not have shut down a 26,000-student college after the initial, early-morning shooting at a campus dormitory. They maintain that a random act of violence such as this is unpreventable. Their campus is like a small city, after all.

But think back to the World Trade Center attacks in 2001. Much of Manhattan -- larger than Blacksburg and certainly the college campus -- was practically shut down after the attacks. The U.S. government halted all commercial airline flights in the U.S. and those coming from other countries.

And you can't shut down a campus with probably 10 streets coming into it and less than half of the enrolled students on campus at any given time? If we can transplant a human heart and put a man on the moon -- with bright students like those at Virginia Tech who accomplish such amazing feats -- you can certainly figure a way to lock down a college campus in an emergency.

In fact, the campus was finally shut down following the massacre. University officials say this is hindsight, however. After all, they mistakenly thought the initial deaths were confined to a domestic spat. And while they didn't want to disrupt the morning classes that day, the entire school has now been closed for almost a week.

A logical response to such limited thinking is to ask how often do two students get shot on a weekday morning in a campus dormitory -- following several tense weeks in which there were two bomb threats. You doubt that gunfire is common on campus, or at least you would hope not for such a prestigious university.

This is not about pointing fingers and assessing blame. There is plenty of blame to be handed out, and that will proceed through the normal channels. This is more of a plea for school officials at all levels to do more than was done at Virginia Tech.

Problematic, disruptive students should be kicked out of school to protect the others. They are not entitled to a college education. And err on the side of caution when a threatening situation arises. Have a plan to address it, complete with preparedness, communication, and coordination.

These types of random, heinous acts will likely continue in our violent society. Preparing for them, and quelling them at the earliest possible moment, will save lives and help deter copycat events.

It certainly could have worked that way at Virginia Tech. The death toll could have stopped at two. Instead, it reached a heartbreaking tally of 32.

They Are Students of Golf /May 2007

Some of the participants in the third-annual "Mad Monday Charity Golf Tournament" last week had to put down their school books -- in order to pick up their golf clubs.

You see, one of the foursomes consisted of students of knowledge, and golf. They were members of the Fernandina Beach High School boys' and girls' golf teams, who got a reprieve from their studies to participate in the tournament sponsored by local real estate agents.

Each year the local high school is invited to enter a team (its entry fee was covered by Old Towne Title this year). And these students came to play. The foursome of Micah Jacobsen, Brad Brogdon, Jillian Spencer and Chelsey Nicklas finished fifth among 36 teams.

But these kids weren't intimidated by the field, or particularly excited about their finish. In fact, they didn't feel they played up to par (or their abilities, in golf parlance). The FBHS team finished a respectable 11-under par, however.

The winning team, sponsored by the News-Leader, shot an eye-watering 21-under par, mostly through the herculean efforts of Joe Parrish and Steve Johnson.

There is something good, and positive, about wholesome community events such as this -- especially when they benefit area charities. It's sort of old style, with exemplary youngsters taking part along with adults.

In this case, maybe it was more "old school."

A Year of Spreading Goodwill   /December 2006

With the local property market taking a bit of a breather from the frenetic pace of recent years, real-estate agents are catching their breath in creative ways.

Some are sharpening their golf game, others are taking personal-development classes, and a select few like Molly Knowlton of Coldwell Banker are setting out on adventurous voyages. As in a 635-mile voyage from Newport, Rhode Island to Bermuda.

Knowlton and an eclectic crew guided a 60-foot sailboat in the 100th-anniversary Newport Bermuda Race in June. The crew included Knowlton and five other Coldwell Banker employees/volunteers, as well as a seasoned captain (who was hired). Some other affiliates also joined in as part of the "Team Coldwell Banker" crew.

Knowlton is no stranger to sailing. She and former husband Bill Kinney lived aboard their own sailboat for years and sailed across the Atlantic Ocean several times.

To be selected as part of the crew, Knowlton needed sailing experience. She had to prove nautical worthiness as part of the selection process. She had done little sailboat racing, but hoped her offshore experience would make up for it.

It did. And on June 15, Knowlton and the 15-member crew (of strangers) left Newport and set out along the ocean route. "We grew as a crew when we were out there," Knowlton said.

They arrived in Bermuda five days later to a joyous champagne toast and hugs. Knowlton served an important role -- as the cook. That meant limited sleep, as she had to have food prepared each time a shift went off duty. On a sailboat in the middle of the ocean, a shift of sailors must always be on duty.

Knowlton and the others had to raise money prior to setting sail. The money was to go to Habitat for Humanity, which is playing an integral role in rebuilding New Orleans and other areas of the Gulf Coast ravaged by recent hurricanes.

Knowlton raised $11,425 in pledges, mostly from businesses in Nassau County. Her boss, Bruce Jasinsky, also helped in the effort with a generous contribution.

But she was not done. She followed the sailing race by taking a trip in November to New Orleans for the annual convention of the National Association of Realtors. There, she volunteered as part of another crew -- who worked on rebuilding houses in the Ninth Ward of New Orleans.

The area, known as "Musicians' Village," provides houses for musicians to live in as they return to New Orleans after the storm. The project is sponsored by Habitat for Humanity, which is Coldwell Bankers' primary charity.

In yet another volunteer role, Knowlton helped place insulation under several of the houses there. It sort of tied it all together. The money Knowlton raised from her sailing trip helped pay for building a Habitat for Humanity house on the Gulf Coast, and then she went there to work on one herself.

"It just capped off the year," Knowlton said. A year of personal voyages, charitable crusades, and something money cannot buy. Good will.

An 'Unhappy' Happy Valley   /June 2011

As a kid, I grew up worshipping Penn State football. The program possessed everything -- sanctity, simplicity, purity.

There was the sanctity of the place they played in, blissfully nicknamed "Happy Valley." It always seemed sunny there on fall afternoons. There was the simplicity of their blue-and-white uniforms with no names, and a coach with black-rimmed glasses who looked like your grandfather.

And there was the purity of a program where the players graduated and no one got into trouble (like at other programs). But like a lot of things in life, something that appeared so perfect and virtuous to a kid turns out to be a mirage. Penn State's football program may be at the top of this list.

The 40 charges against former defensive coordinator Jerry Sandusky (who is 67 years old) are sickening enough -- that he purportedly started a foundation for troubled boys and then abused them. Worse yet, some of it supposedly happened on the Penn State campus, even though he was not a coach then.

These days, football and basketball programs are brought to their knees by a singular recruiting violation, or, in rival Ohio State's instance, when a coach hid the truth about his players bartering memorabilia for tattoos.

In this instance, there is a belief that other coaches at Penn State had learned something unusual was going on years ago, including head coach Joe Paterno. It is being reported that Paterno feels exonerated because he forwarded his suspicions to the athletic director.

This is not like hosting a cook-out at your house and inviting recruits. This is nothing like your players trading their jerseys for tattoos. If true, this is like no other.

Yeah, we all know that in our system everyone gets his say in court, that you are not guilty until a judge convicts you that way. But these charges and graphic accounts are so disgraceful and despicable that damage is already done.

Investigators can't fabricate things like this. They have 23 pages of evidence from a grand jury investigation, according to reports. If true, the Penn State football program must be completely dismantled, and the slate wiped clean. Maybe then it can rebuild its reputation.

For a kid, it would be more disturbing than finding out your best friend was cheating you. I have always rooted for Penn State football. Now, like a lot of others, I will always root against them -- if these charges are accurate.

Some people just root against the good guys. Like with Tim Tebow. He is true and pure, and people can't stand it. Paterno was always like that as a coach.

This shakes your confidence in people. Forget the millions of dollars that Penn State football and other big-time programs bring to their schools. This is about adults mentoring impressionable kids. This is about what is right, and what is wrong.

If anything was ever wrong with sports, it would be this. Even though Paterno holds the record for most coaching victories in major college football, he would have a disclaimer of morality by his name. Victories just don't matter compared to this.

A few Penn State officials have stepped down for allegedly misleading authorities as to what they knew. There will be more fallout, to be sure. And there should be, regardless who it is.

You wonder what is sacred these days. Hallowed enough for kids to believe in. As the head football coach, Paterno cultivated "a reputation for putting integrity ahead of modern college-sports economics," according to one news report.

But not now, not being associated with what would be the worst scandal in the history of college sports. So sorry to Joe "Pa" as he is reverently known for being a father figure.

Happy days are hardly here again in Happy Valley. Worse yet, happy days have become horrid days – in this sickening saga.

(Note: Excerpts from this column will be used in a book currently being written by a professor emeritus at Penn State University on this topic. The book, "Pandora's Box in Happy Valley: The Jerry Sandusky Scandal," is the work of Ronald A. Smith, who had worked as a professor at Penn State and saw first-hand the emergence of the Nittany Lion football team and its once-celebrated coach, Joe Paterno.)

The Spirit of Ned Tyson   /November 2010

It was a cold winter day several years ago, when Ned Tyson had a warm thought.

Let's hold a running race each year in February to attract people to Amelia Island -- when tourist traffic is normally slow. This would help put Amelia Island on the map of the running circles, and help local businesses trying to endure the agonies of the off-season.

Ned called together Joe Gerrity and me for lunch at Sliders' Seaside Restaurant. He pitched his idea. We agreed it could be a home run -- but that we could also whiff. That's all the hope Ned needed.

He launched into high gear, contacting city officials and the Pirates Club and the high school. He would make this a community event. Gerrity helped with the coordination and logistics; I handled publicity; and Ned did the rest.

City officials quickly embraced the idea (due to Ned's enthusiasm and salesmanship and reputation). The police were onboard, offering to navigate the roadways. The Pirates Club would bring in its big wooden ship for local flavor, and line the race course in costume to encourage the runners. The cheerleaders from the high school would bring their enthusiasm, and the honors students would handle the registration and water tables.

In his fastidious preparation, Ned rode his bike along the 6.2-mile race course many times to ensure its accuracy and appeal. He wanted the event woven into the historic fabric of the city. And he liked the ring and symbolism of the name he penned, "Pirates on the Run."

The first race came together with surprising ease. We had 70 runners -- including local favorite Ryder Leary. The seed had been planted.

It would blossom into a race of 700 runners today, nurtured in recent years by the ever-capable hands of the Amelia Island Runners club. Ned had planned to pass the baton as the race grew in size. However, it would never have been born without him.

The race would become another of Ned's accomplishments in the fitness and wellness arenas. He ran a successful health fair at the Amelia Island Plantation for years. He pioneered a walking club on the island, and brought in an expert to speak about it.

Ned was committed to the benefits of exercise for everyone -- regardless of age, fitness level, or motivation. He saw it as critical to keeping down the costs of health care for his clients and the insurance industry as a whole. And he orchestrated a new health care facility for school employees in the county in a last-gasp attempt to control costs.

If Ned wasn't helping people, he was thinking about it. His contribution to our community will be ever-lasting. It is with a sad, tragic irony that someone who so capably and tirelessly campaigned for good health would lose his life to a rare disease like ALS.

But whenever you see someone walking or running or exercising in some way, they are advancing his life's work and legacy. With each stride, with each regenerative breath, with each bead of sweat, Ned Tyson's spirit lives, and endures.

An Investment of a Different Kind   /May 2009

This article is a little different than usual. But so is the subject.

It's about an investment that keeps on giving -- and taking. It's about a bond that is not financial in nature, but instead emotional. A bond that forms quicker and stronger than epoxy, and fosters a lifetime of blissful experiences.

This is the bond between a father and a daughter. Fathers raise daughters differently than they do sons. It's probably not fair or equitable. But it's justifiable to a dad, because of this spiritual union.

Fathers and daughters can laugh together and cry together. They try to make sense of a complicated world, distilling moments in time into something precious. Together you frolic when you should behave, and whisper when you should be quiet. Rules are boundaries that don't always apply when you're together and having fun.

As a father, you invest your time into your relationship as willingly and tirelessly as Warren Buffet invests money. The return you get is unparalleled. A warm smile or a sweet utterance of "Daddy" is sufficient payment for your time.

You are indescribably proud. You see yourself in her actions and mannerisms and speech. Sometimes, you wonder if this is good, recalling what you've seen and done in your past.

The investment part begins early. You never imagined that children's clothing could cost so much. Then there are dolls to buy and teeth to straighten. And paying for cars and college.

College is a mountain of an expense. Tuitions are increasing by 7 percent a year on average -- even in a recession -- while room-and-board costs grow like the U.S. national debt or the population of China.

And more students are attending college than ever, when you consider the foreign influx. In Florida, state universities and community colleges are bursting with enrollments and new construction on their campuses.

Scholarships and grants can help, as do unsurpassed in-state offerings such as Bright Futures and the Florida Prepaid Program.

For Florida high school graduates, the costs of college are defrayed through the state's emphasis on higher education and programs such as these.

Fernandina Beach High School will hold its graduation this week for several hundred seniors. My daughter will be among them. She is the student body president.

Another contingent of bright-eyed and ambitious students will partake in the hallowed passage to the workplace or college. It is sentimental for parents, but long-anticipated for students.

Graduation is a time for reflection, and a time for dreaming. Reach for the stars and a bright future, but don't forget your past. Growing up in the enchanted environment of Fernandina Beach will be one of your fondest memories.

After graduation, the close-knit circle of friends unravels, as everyone chases their dreams. But you'll keep your high school friends for life, as you will the lessons from your teachers.

As a father, the most exhilarating thing is that this story is just beginning. Many new and riveting chapters will be written in coming years, adding to a bulging scrapbook of memories -- for a father and his daughter.

<u>Appendix</u>

Steve Nicklas/Biography

☐   April 2008 to August 2011: First Vice President/Broker-in-Charge of UBS Financial Services office in Fernandina Beach.

☐   June 2001 to April 2008: First Vice President/Investments for Prudential/Wachovia Securities in Ponte Vedra Beach.

☐   February 1998 to June 2001: Broker-in-Charge of Morgan Stanley office in Fernandina Beach.

☐   March 1994 to February 1998: Associate Vice President for Smith Barney in Jacksonville.

☐   1994 to present: Authored "All About Money" and "Steve's Marketplace" financial columns for the New York Times Regional Newspaper Group as well as Community Newspapers, Inc. Financial columns appear regularly in Fernandina Beach News-Leader, Nassau County Record, and (Jacksonville) Beaches Leader.

☐   February 2001 to present: Instructor of "Investing in Today's Financial Markets" at Florida Community College of Jacksonville and Florida State College.

☐   1995 to 2005: Co-hosted "Money Talk" financial show on AM-1460 and performed business reports for National Public Radio's Stereo 90-FM, both in Jacksonville, as well as for several radio stations in Fernandina Beach.

☐   Attended Texas Christian University, The College of New Jersey and Thomas Edison State College in Trenton, NJ.

Steve Nicklas visiting the floor of the New York Stock Exchange –
a true thrill for any financial advisor.

Another visit to the New York Stock Exchange – and an opportunity to ring the opening bell (strictly ceremonial, however).

Standing on the field of the Miami Dolphins' stadium with my brother, Mark Nicklas, as guests of Sun Life Financial. Ironically, the Dolphins lost the game to the Denver Broncos – in the first comeback victory for QB Tim Tebow.

43865211R00086

Made in the USA
Middletown, DE
21 May 2017